GOD
Where Are You?
It's Me!

TRACY L CLARK

10-10-10
Publishing

GOD Where Are You? It's Me!

www.tracylclark.com

ISBN: 978-1-77277-398-9

Publisher
10-10-10 Publishing
Markham, ON
Canada

Printed in Canada and the United States of America

Dedication

I dedicate this book to my two incredible daughters, Nina and Christina. Without them in my life, I wouldn't have chosen to keep going and would have left the planet once and for all.

For everyone who reads this book, I dedicate this to your journey, and hope that you'll see the greatness within you! Please remember, you are a child of God, and you are here for greatness. Trust, Know, and Believe that you have a divine mission and purpose. Once you fully believe it, God will open doors that you never could have imagined possible!

Table of Contents

Acknowledgements   vii
Foreword   ix

Chapter 1
When You Did Not Ask for the Life You Got   **1**
What's Your Story?   11

Chapter 2
The Me Realm: Unleash Your Superhuman Within   **17**
Open New Doorways by Asking Why   26
Getting Started   32

Chapter 3
Piece by Piece, Step by Step, From Agony to Joy   **37**
My Body Turned Black From Blocked Blood Flow   40
From the Jesus Moment to a New Life   46
This is Not a Pity Party   50

Chapter 4
It Started in Las Vegas; I Believed and I Received   **55**
Trust and Follow the Signs   59

Chapter 5
The Mind is a Virus!   **71**
Taking Back Control of Your Mind   77
Who Has the Password to Your Mental Wi-Fi?   78

Chapter 6

Stop Cursing Your Life; You're on the Brink of a Miracle!   **87**

Cursing My Life   88

Seeing Through the Pain   93

Don't Give Up Before the Miracle Arrives!   99

Chapter 7

Let Go of Fear to Rebuild Your Foundation   **107**

What to Do if You Don't Know Any Better   120

Rebuilding Your Foundation   124

The Time Has Come to Choose   131

Chapter 8

The Power of Gratitude and the Power of Giving   **135**

Gratitude is Not Just Lip Service   139

Giving With Joy, Not Obligation   141

Sharing is Not Always Caring   145

Simple Things to Do Right Now to Change Your Life   150

Chapter 9

Radical Faith, Radical Trust   **161**

Finding Faith When Young   163

Faith versus Religion   168

Make the Choice!   175

Chapter 10

Follow the Energy   **181**

Peeling off the Layers   183

Even More Layers to Go   185

Choosing to Forgive   187

Chapter 11

The Force   **197**

Darkness is Seductive   201

Acknowledgements

My thanks to Olga Arsenyuk, who took me under her wing when I was scared and unsure of what to do next on my journey. Olga taught me that I wasn't crazy, and helped me along my path. If not for her teachings and guidance, I would not be where I am today. I thank you Olga, from the bottom of my heart, and I know that you are always watching over me from the heavens.

Thank you to all of my clients who allowed me to share my gifts with them, and for believing in me each and every day to help guide the way with the God of their understanding.

To the TLC Community, that has come together to support everyone in wonderful and miraculous ways, I love you all so much and I am so thankful for the opportunity to watch each of you grow and shine with clarity in the life of your dreams.

My final thanks is to the Hand of God for pulling me out of the dark when I kept going back in and for showing me every day that miracles do exist!

Foreword

How many foxhole prayers have you said in your lifetime? Can you remember when you hit a rock bottom and thought, "Who will help me? Is there a power out there that even knows I exist?"

By the time I read the first ten pages of this book, I thought, "Is this the Tracy L Clark that does a powerful, uplifting, transformative radio show each week? How did she survive?" Then . . . another thought emerged: "She was born to tell this story." What would you do if there was no limit to what you could achieve, regardless of the pain of your past? There is no guessing when it comes to this book. Tracy holds up a mirror to your pain and problems, but offers a massive paradigm roadmap to help you shift, grow, and transform.

Life is a complex amalgamation of experiences, good and bad. These experiences teach us about ourselves, and how we fit into the world around us. Whether we realize it or not, these experiences limit us just as much as we grow from them, if not more so. Too often, failure and pain create a locked door, preventing us from exploring certain facets of ourselves, or our connections to the world around us. Our struggles become a prison that traps us, restricting us from reaching out to grab everything that the universe has to offer.

Early in my life, I succumbed to this limiting world view, believing there are negative forces beyond my control that impacted my very being. As soon as I perceived myself losing control, I actively gave up trying to get it back and sought the comfort of whatever I could to numb myself. I began to close in on myself, to ignore all the possibilities that I had once aimed for. This mental and emotional pressure took a toll on my physical health as well, which clouded my vision even further. The connection between the mind and the body is something that we do not fully understand — it is perhaps more powerful than we can comprehend. I became stuck in my ways and scared of any change that might disrupt this. For no matter how bad I thought my life was, it still felt comfortable and predictable — and the unknown did not.

Taking that initial leap of faith into something new was scary, but I had gotten to a point where the fear of staying still felt worse. I cannot remember the exact moment when I knew I had to change, but I like to think that I had already subconsciously started the process before I could consciously understand it. The universe had been giving me signs all along, and I believe I was searching for them before I even knew what they were for. Trusting my faith when I had once doubted it was difficult, but by this point, I could already feel it working.

Consider this tipping point that Tracy once faced, and take it in.

I thought to myself, "Tracy, what do you want to do? Do you want to sell your soul to the devil and go back to that world full of snakes and idiots, or do you really want to follow your passion?"

Have you not faced a similar choice, when you knew that your reality did not align with your right path? It can be difficult to muster up the courage to even face the question, to admit that you have somehow been led astray from what was meant to be. If not until today, well . . . Now is the time to trust.

It was Tracy L Clark who reminded me of the true strength we all have, through this transformative book. Tracy is the perfect example of someone who has trusted in her faith and has been rewarded. She has lived a life that has been full of struggle, but she refused to let it stop her.

From birth, she was dealt a hand that would have caused many people to fold, to give up, to walk away from ever trying anything new again. And yet, she persevered. Despite three near-death experiences, Tracy is living her life to the absolute fullest. Her will to live is a testament to the strength of the power of her body and her internal energy that cannot be dimmed.

When I first met Tracy, I could never have known how much pain and suffering she had once faced. She hosts her show on our network, The Transformation Network, and has always been a continuous source of positive energy. She treats every day as if it were a blessing, and as if she has never experienced failure. Anything has always been possible to her, and success is inevitable. Her never-ending positivity seems to attract good things from the universe, in all shapes and sizes. Just being around her energy was enough to make me feel as though I was in close proximity to an unseen power beyond my understanding. Through *Hey God, Are You There, It's Me,* Tracy details her journey, and how she has learned to believe in the power of her own mind. Tracy is proof that you can achieve the unimaginable when you let go of preconceived restrictions, and refuse to let external forces affect your internal light.

Your mind is the key to unlocking your full potential, but it is also the one thing that is really holding you back. In a world that seems full of restrictions, it is important to remember the true power of the self. We often wait too long for help from external sources, forgetting that we can achieve so much more by ourselves. Change starts from within the mind. This book will teach you all that you need to know in order to unlock your true potential, so that you can manifest success beyond what you may have thought possible. Disregarding your existing beliefs can be difficult, but with the right guidance, it will ultimately lead you to your right path.

Faith looks and feels different to each person, but its fundamental purpose is to offer us the strength we need. Tracy refers to "the God of my understanding," as the spiritual entity that gives her strength. Regardless of our personal and unique beliefs, there is a universal force that is guiding us. How you envision this force is completely up to you, because your power is not dictated by your perception of it, but rather by your overwhelming faith that it can change your life.

Today Tracy and I share many things in common, including one counterintuitive experience. People think we are "too happy." Perhaps as mentors, coaches, speakers, people in the public, we can't possibly know their pain. It seems unrealistic that folks like us could have ever felt the pain of another. But that is the brilliance of Tracy's story and this book. Despite all the loss, struggle, illness, roadblocks, fatal relationships, I echo Tracy's message in this book and in her life:

I tell them I am sorry, but I am not going to be unhappy just to appease them. I know what misery is like; I lived a miserable life for many years, and I don't need to hang out there anymore . . . Happiness is contagious, and you should always take as much as you can get. Not to mention, happiness allows God to bring more miracles because on a vibrational scale it attracts your desires faster than fear or anger.

If you have picked up this book, it is because you are ready to make the change necessary to grow. You want to believe and trust that you too can laugh in the face of fear or trauma. You want to be free from the shackles of unfulfilled dreams, empty promises, so you can feel the inspiration for life that you once felt. You have searched outside yourself and perhaps thought there are no people "out there" who could possibly understand your journey or even your loss of any spiritual connection. I did too!

It can be painful and terrifying to let go of what feels comfortable, even if it no longer serves you. But it will be worth it. Unlearning every harmful pattern of behavior you have been taught is taxing and will take time, but it gives you the freedom to consider other choices you might have previously ignored. With no limitations, you are capable of creating the life that you want, not the life you must settle for. If this seems impossible today, remember this one lesson that Tracy has learned so very well:

"The difficulties are not meant to defeat you; they are meant to promote you. Don't give up; you're about to be promoted!!"

So as you turn each page of this book, you will discover a truth that has been forgotten. You will begin to focus on yourself with a new respect, and the love of God/the Universe will flow through the new you. The very essence of your cells will call to regenerate in a powerful way. You may also realize that you are much more powerful than you ever imagined as you walk the transformative journey, step by step with Tracy, as you turn each page.

When there is no limit to what you can achieve, you can achieve it all.

—Dr. Pat Baccili, Ph.D.
Host of The Dr. Pat Show
CEO, The Transformation Network and
Transformation Talk Radio

Throughout this book, you will read testimonials from all over the world. They are placed in the book so that you can take the energy that is behind their creative miracles.

Testimonials are away for you to share what the Hand of God is doing in your life so that others can enjoy the blessings!

Read the testimonial and say, "Thank you God, I am taking that energy too!"

Watch the miracles unfold in your life!

Chapter 1

When You Did Not Ask for the Life You Got

"Things don't happen to you, they happen for you!"

— Tracy L Clark

I came into this world in pretty rough shape!

I was born with a concave chest cavity, called pectus excavatum, which left a deep depression in my chest. My legs and hips were detached from my body, which meant that I required a cast to hold everything in place. To make matters even worse, my nervous system was extremely damaged and I lived with excruciating pain throughout much of my life.

For 6 weeks after my birth, I projectile vomited every bit of food that was fed to me. I couldn't keep any of it down and as a newborn, I was so deprived of much-needed nutrients that I became emaciated. I was an 8-lb baby but after weeks of not being able to absorb the food, I became severely malnourished.

We lived in a small gold mining town in Manitoba called Flin Flon, and the hospital wasn't very sophisticated. No one could seem to figure out what the issue was and they just decided to keep giving me medicine to see if it would fix itself.

My mother was led to the family health clinic where there was a doctor visiting from the big city who quickly seemed to figure out the issue. I had a condition called pyloric stenosis, this is where the stomach valve is sealed shut and cannot allow food to pass through. It is a condition that would now be caught quickly, but back then it was not as common in girls as it was in boys. Due to the lack of food, they had to open the valve and start to put fluids into my body.

With no vein to poke in my arms, the only solution was to strap me to the bed to feed me through my head. This form of feeding wasn't ideal for a young baby but I was so emaciated that they couldn't find a vein, and most people thought that I was going to die. When I was barely two months old, I underwent surgery to open up the valve.

I suffered croup, asthma, bronchitis and severe allergies from the time I was born and I eventually had to have an inhaler everywhere that I went. Sometimes, until I was a young teenager, I even had to go on a machine to increase my ability to breathe.

Eventually, I said enough is enough—I wasn't aware at the time that I was making the first connections to my body, and I did not even realize what I was doing by connecting to my body.

At three, my mom, my older sister, and I were kicked out of the family home. My parents' marriage was ending and my dad did not have the best relationship coping skills. My parents were very young and not many people at that age have proper coping skills. My dad moved his girlfriend in while my mom was away and like any good mother would, as soon as she heard about the girlfriend she hopped on a plane and came back to retrieve us.

I remember my dad's girlfriend and my mom slugging it out in a huge fight and the next thing that I knew, we were out of the house. We left with garbage bags of clothes in hand. I blocked out most of what happened after that but I do remember that we travelled 8 hours from our small town to a big city, scared and unsure of what was happening.

Every one one of us was afraid of the future, as everything that we knew was unravelling at light speed. Many tears and many nightmares were to come at such a young age.

No one can really understand the consequences of their actions until many years later. However, it is clear that an action always has a reaction, good or bad.

We ended up in a shelter of some sort, and the next day my sister Kim and I woke up with a red rash that quickly developed into chickenpox. We eventually moved to low-income housing, as my mom ended up on welfare with no support and no family around to help. Losing my home so suddenly, which was my foundation of stability, brought to me a cutting sense of loss which seeped deep into my body.

Clearly my body did not want to see any more, as many days I would wake up with my eyes sealed shut. So much gunk was coming out of them that I would feel my way to the bathroom to find a warm wet towel to wash away the bacteria that was keeping them closed. Eyes will do this when you simply have no desire to see any more! My eyes at a young age clearly said "No more!"

I grew up always feeling unsafe. As a young and sensitive child who was an empath, I absorbed my mother's worries and fears about money, and how she would take care of us, as well as her own broken heart and heartache.

When I was five, I suffered tummy pains that were so severe that I doubled up in agony. It felt like someone had knifed me in the stomach. It was later discovered that I had stomach ulcers, diverticulitis, and irritable bowel syndrome.

I remember the day that they had to take tests, I had to sit in the cold hospital x-ray room all by myself. Unfortunately, I was scared, in tears, and in pain, and I was unwilling to take the awful drink that they gave me to prepare me for the x-rays.

Looking back, I realize that it must have contained a dye so that they could see where the blockages were but it smelled funny and tasted bad, so I refused to drink it. I sobbed so hard that the doctor came out of his office and told me to "Quit your whining, just drink that!"

A kind nurse—yes, an earth angel—rose to my defence but the encounter carved within me my dislike of authority figures. The environment was loud and angry, and it was totally frightening! It didn't appear that they could fully treat my stomach pain, and I had to run to the bathroom all of the time. I doubled over after every meal, feeling suffocated because I couldn't breathe.

We continued in this way and this became my new normal.

At five, while riding my bike, I was crossing the road and a car turned the corner and collided right into me.

Bang! I somersaulted into the air, hit the roof of the car, rolled down its side, and landed in the middle of the road. The people who were gathered around the accident were certain that I would die. I was rushed to the hospital and I remember being more worried about how much of a wreck my bike was and how embarrassing it was that I had peed in my pants.

It was definitely traumatic, and this was yet another instance when I wanted to leave my body and check out. Evidently earth school was not for me, clearly the universe was telling me that it was time to go, but it never happened.

Soon after the accident, me, my sister, and a friend, were kidnapped by a paedophile.

I recall seeing a young man, around 18–19 years old, riding his bike in our neighbourhood. There was something that was aberrant about him and my young five-year-old self kept saying to my mom, "I don't trust him! I don't feel safe when I see him."

My mom didn't pay a whole lot of attention to my concerns but because I was very sensitive, intuitive, and empathetic, I was extremely uneasy.

Me and my 7-year-old sister, who is two years older than I am, would often be taken care of by another lady when my mom was busy. She would babysit us at her own residence. Her young daughter was 7 years old.

The daughter was an afterthought to her parents and was born late in their lives—her brothers, all of whom were bikers, were already nearly 20 years old.

This young girl Jackie was savvy and tough, and it was her street smarts that saved us from an ugly fate.

All three of us were playing hide-and-seek in the park. We were near some bushes when the guy, of whom I was highly suspicious, dashed out of hiding and grabbed me.

I screamed! My sister and our friend came running towards me but then he grabbed all three of us. He bundled us into the basement of a house that was undergoing construction, pointing his gun at us to deter any attempts at escape.

Clearly, he was intending to rape all of us, starting with our friend, the biker girl. Pointing a gun at my sister, he pressed her to undress our friend. Meanwhile, we were all terrified and were crying bitterly. His dog was barking and he was screaming at us to keep quiet.

Thankfully, biker girl had her wits about her, and she whispered to my sister, "Pretend you are taking off my top. Pretend! I'm going to run and get help" . . . and she did!

She ran away from the house so fast and the paedophile took off after her yelling hoarsely "Come back here!"

Meanwhile, my sister grabbed the opportunity to climb out of the dugout. She tried to pull me up but I was so small and fragile that I just didn't have enough body strength to pull myself up.

We could see that the paedophile was coming back, so my sister took one look at me and said, "Hang in there, I'm going to get help! I'll come back, I'll come back!"

I was left alone with the would-be rapist. When he got back to the basement he kept screaming at me, "Where did they go? Where did they go?" He was madder than a hornet! Meanwhile with my intense dislike of loud, angry voices, I was so wrapped up in terror and fear that I was rooted to where I stood and I was crying. He continued screaming at me and he ordered his dog to bite chunks off of me. He grabbed me by my pony tail, threw me face down on the ground, and put a gun to my head. I could hear the distant sounds of police sirens just before I blacked out.

Little did I know about the years of trauma that would come from this event. It was like no one wanted to talk about it. No one understood the pain, the trauma, and the fear of going outside again. I remember always looking around, waiting to see if someone else was going to pop out from around the corner.

Sleeping was horrible! I would lie in my bed and pile hundreds of stuffed animals on top of myself, in the hopes that they would keep me hidden from the boogie men. I would cry a lot at night but never left my room. I never felt as alone or scared as I did at that time.

On some level, I also started to realize that I was on my own. I would need to learn how to do everything on my own and trust NO ONE! I would rely on no one and figure everything out for myself. At such a young age, a new safety program had been created deep within me.

Trust me when I say that this led to many roadblocks as I started to grow into a young adult.

At the age of 7, I was back in the hospital for severe allergies. Through doing allergy testing on my back, they found that my immune system reacted to just about everything as an invasion on the body.

From my perspective as an adult, I am not surprised that this happened. The turbulent energies and emotions, which were stirred up from the kidnapping attempt, were repressed because my parents couldn't bring themselves to discuss it with me.

My body couldn't cope with all of the stored-up terror and it started to shut down.

I needed to get a serum at the hospital to minimize the allergy attacks. A nurse gave me the first injection and my eyes immediately rolled into the back of my head. I remember falling down before everything turned black.

When I came to, I was in a gown in a hospital bed. My chest hurt badly and all that I wanted was to get back to the dark and peaceful place where I had been just before waking up. I had no problem not coming back to this earth because life was so punishing. My mom learned much later that the hospital staff had to crash-cart me to revive my heart, which had stopped beating because of a severe reaction to the serum.

It was during that brief space in time that I left my body. I had realized that I was not for this world. The enemy spirit had a clear agenda: remove this child before she grows up! I did not realize that I was in a battle between the dark and the light until much later in life.

I had two more near-death experiences (NDE) in my adult years. The second one took place when I gave birth to my second daughter and almost checked out on the operating table. The third NDE happened when I was at home.

Without any warning, I left my body and went to a realm with indescribably beautiful colours, sharp clarity, and all-encompassing love. I immersed myself in the beautiful bliss and peace, and I so badly wanted to stay because I was pain-free.

However, I kept hearing a voice that said, "You have to go back. You have to go back to your kids. You've got to go back!" Suddenly there was extremely loud music, that I have never heard replicated again, and colours that were not of this world!

I was loving every minute of it, and I heard once again, "You must go back! It is not your time!" and I was ejected out of the ethereal realm and back into my body.

This last NDE was a wake-up call for me. As much as I wanted to leave behind the fears, grief, loss, and physical pain, which made up my whole life, I had to take responsibility for what was happening to me because leaving this earthly plane would mean abandoning my two young daughters. I eventually realized that this was NOT an option, so I needed to change my course of action!

I have often mused that had I known that my life would unfold in such a particularly painful way, I would have strongly resisted coming through the birth canal. Just like a victim in a horror movie that is being dragged feet first to a fate worse than death, I would have dug my unformed baby nails into the walls of my mother's womb and put up a fierce fight. I would have checked out at the point of birth to avoid the unforeseen traumas that would follow.

The fears of abandonment, the dread of scarcity, being terrified of the world, the pervasive feeling of being unsafe, the excruciating physical pains, the illnesses from a warped DNA, the bullying through school because of my body and head shakes, and the terrors of being kidnapped and almost raped—all of these compounded traumas and their associated emotions were trapped within my body.

The emotions interconnected and intersected and formed an intricate web that lodged itself in various parts of my body, which found its way to the surface as even more illnesses.

It manifested as the seizure-like uncontrollable shaking of my eyes, my arms, and my head. This was so painful that I wanted to rip out the spots of pain and tear off my head just to stop the excruciating agony!

It came out as respiratory difficulties because I couldn't breathe in life in all of its beauty and joys, along with its messiness and its lessons. I was being smothered by its pain!

The first imprints and patterning of abandonment and loss were created by my parents' divorce and our sudden eviction from our home. These were reinforced later when the adults in the room couldn't bring themselves to talk about my kidnapping. As a highly sensitive child, I needed a lot of love and care.

Instead, after the police hauled the paedophile away, my mom and my stepfather sent me off to bed. I tried to talk to my mom about it but she couldn't deal with the entire incident. She only added that one of the cops had indicated that had it been his daughter, he wouldn't have called the cops on the kidnapper, he would have dealt with it himself!

In my room, I spent so much time hiding, sad and angry! As the tears etched tracks on my cheeks, tracks of pain were being etched on my inner self. I was good at pretending that all was okay. Good at pretending that I had it taken care of, good at pretending that I could figure it all out, I was good at PRETENDING!

This is not meant to be a litany of woes! On the contrary, I have listed my experiences to demonstrate that just because you've been dealt a bad hand in life doesn't mean that is what you are stuck with, nor that you should have to accept it as your cross to bear.

You can change, you can transform, and you can make the deep shifts at lightning speed! You don't have to go through interminable sessions of body work, or nutrition counselling, or visits to the doctor. I know because I have done it—against seemingly loaded odds!

However, you must be ready, you must make yourself a priority, and you must be willing to make some massive changes that will hurt like hell and make you feel crazy at times. You must be willing to unlearn all that you have learned and never look back!

After multiple trips to many doctors, the consensus was that the bobble-head shaking was a neurological defect that I would have to live with for the rest of my life. I was incessantly bullied at school for my ragdoll motions. The weight of peer disapproval ate into my self-esteem, I was afraid to speak up for fear of being yelled at, and I was terrified to step into who I was and who I wanted to be.

Once I understood how buried emotions can affect our way of being, I healed myself.

The first thing that I did was stop the shaking in my arms and my eyes. It took a little longer for the head movements to stop but I had the unshakeable faith, and the deep knowing in my core, that I would get to that point—I would correct it one day—and I did!

Spirit led me to the right osteopath and it only took one treatment! I have never had a head shake since!

Transformation is right within your grasp! You have to take responsibility and you have to be committed to healing yourself!

My Body Regeneration Method™, which is channelled through me by God, gives you simple tools and some words to speak. Just as importantly, you need to have faith in the realm of unlimited possibilities, where you move from limited to limitless!

Have you ever wondered why you came to this planet? Have you thought that there must be more to life than just working for a salary, paying taxes, saving for retirement, and then dying? I am sure you have looked around your world many times, seen the stress that you and your friends carry, within and without, and thought to yourself, "This can't be all that life is about!" If you've asked yourself why you are here, what the reason is for your being, and how you can create a life in which you thrive, rather than one in which you are simply going through the motions, you have come to the right place!

What's Your Story?

Everyone has a story, and it's that story that moulds, shifts, and shapes us into who we are. We've been conditioned in our lives to believe it's our traumas and hurtful events that make us who we are. We are conditioned to wallow in the pain of the past, to talk about it over and over again, to sit in it, and to believe that the hurt would never go away.

We get so attached to our pain that it becomes familiar, and it becomes our friend! It is something with which we know how to deal.

When we become the subject of other people's pity, we get a pass in life because the more that we play up the suffering, the more the people around us will say "Poor you!"

Rather than using tools to detach from the shackles of the emotions and transmuting the pain to unlock our hidden powers and dimensions, we leverage the pain to get a free pass from doing our inner work, like we would get a day off of school or from work.

But what's the cost of this wallowing to you?

You'll always stay trapped in your sorrows, anguish, and agony, and you won't be able to access the joyful elevated realities that become available to someone else who is willing to evict the emotions that hamper a full life.

When you are able to speak about the past without feeling the grief, or the fear, or the rage somewhere in your body, that's your healing!

When you have the mental strength to stand up to your emotions and declare, "You're not my master but we can be allies!" you'll be able to consciously choose what you want to allow into your reality.

Your emotions are guideposts to show you where you are stuck and what's keeping you locked down in that stasis. They are not your master, and when you pay attention to where the difficulties and the pain are stuck, you reveal to yourself the opportunities to heal, to grow, and to expand!

Have you secretly ached for superpowers like those possessed by the Marvel superheroes you see on the screen? Have you yearned to be able to fight off bullets with golden cuffs on your wrists, raise spaceships out of a swamp with just the strength of your intention, or heal yourself of pain with a few taps on your body like the Kung Fu fighters would?

What if I told you that within you there are superpowers? —supernatural abilities that have been gifted to you by Spirit! Powers that you can plug into to heal yourself!

Some of you may be dismissing what I am saying as hogwash: "There's no such thing as miracles!" you may say.

I would respond, "How about reframing that perspective?" Miracles are all around us! A butterfly metamorphosing from a caterpillar is a miracle! A baby is a miracle! The fact that we are all anchored to this beautiful Earth instead of flailing into space is a miracle! That the sun rises in the morning and sets at night daily, without fail, is a miracle!

You are a miracle! . . . and once you step up to admitting the fact that you've been gifted by Spirit, you can tap into your superhuman abilities!

Many now call me the "Body Whisperer" because the God of my understanding started to guide me and show me the way to a new way of living, and a new way of being!

I am just the conduit, Spirit does all the work!

I previously mentioned that I needed an inhaler for my asthma until I was 13. What happened at that age, was that one day when I was inserting the medication into the inhaler, I started shaking with anger.

I'd had enough of my dependence upon the inhaler, so I declared to it, with all of the fervour a teenager can summon up: "I am done with this! I don't have asthma; I am getting rid of you! I evict you out of my body! "

I never touched my inhaler again, because with my words and my strong intention, I had evicted the asthma from my energy field. I didn't recognize my strength at that time and I didn't understand the powers that were dormant within me until much later.

I have included this story in here to show that you don't have to wait till you are all grown-up and wise to the ways of the world to begin tapping into your superhuman powers. You just have to pay attention and be willing to discard the old beliefs and structures that don't serve you!

I did not understand until much later that something much bigger than myself was working with me to remove these enemy forces and open my eyes to a new way of existing.

God works in mysterious ways, and you must trust it will never be the way that you think!

They call me "The Body Whisperer" because I transformed my whole life for the better when many experts, for 32 years, had written me off and condemned me to a cage of illnesses.

I repaired and restored myself by understanding the crucial need to listen to the body, to delete old programming, and to instil a new way of understanding the body.

Many people choose to ignore the messages from the body until they are sick, or until they are out of work, or until they are dealing with the heartbreak of a failed relationship.

I beg you, don't allow this to be you! It is a much harder journey to travel down that road— trust me!

My journey was the reverse; I was born deathly sick. I learned to listen and I healed! I learned to listen to the whispers that were being seeded to me that I had not heard before.

Join me, and together we will journey to a new you!

As you read these pages, you will be gifted and imparted with words of power that will touch the depths of your soul! They will stir up your latent gifts so that you will realize the dreams that you dare to dream, embrace the innate power that was given to you by Spirit, and consciously and intentionally design an expanded, inspired, and fulfilling life!

We will unleash the superhuman within and together, the power of the Hand of God will show you a new way of living, and enable you to leave the world of merely existing!

Testimonial 1:
Healing That Saved My Life

Hi Tracy,

I hope you're having a great day!

A few years back, I started working with you, and my life and health has improved so much. I was having my darkest days, back in 2017, where suicide was the only way I thought I'd ever shake the ball of demons that would choose to try and destroy me. But I fought back, and with your help then, you guided me to where I needed to be in regards to my hysterectomy; and again, with your healing and shifting, I made it, and I feel so much better. But I was still sick, and you knew this. Once I finally opened up and put it all in God's hands, I found out that it was my implants; they were literally killing me, with the poison seeping into my system. You told me to be patient and that it would all be okay. Well, here I am, 23 days later, and the doctors cannot believe how well I have healed and how much better I look and feel. They asked me what vitamins I'm using. I said, "Tracy L Clark." I know I have a ways to go; it's a process. But I am smiling through it. You have helped my husband immensely, and my children. I can never ever thank you enough for that. They are my life, and seeing them benefit from you and your amazing gift, fills my heart more than ever. The other night, when you were doing clearing for all of us, my brother came home and said that he felt like something had just been shed from him. I never spoke about this because he and my mom are a little resistant to this, but anyhow, he said it must be planetary and spirit. I almost fell off my chair! That's a win for you. And my mom has been trying to sell her motorhome for 3 years, and it is finally sold—yay!! So much happening over here, and I am excited for what's to come.

P.S. You literally saved my life. Forever grateful, God bless you, and much love from the Russell family.

xoxo

Chapter 2

The Me Realm:
Unleash Your Superhuman Within

"Stop overthinking! You are not stuck, it is all in your mind!"

— Tracy L Clark

Do you love a good sci-fi movie or long-running TV shows such as Supernatural? Are you drawn to movies where angels come down to our reality and save the helpless and heal the ill? Have you longed to be like an angel? To reach out, touch someone, and instantly heal that person!

Have you ever asked yourself why so many people tune in to Netflix or TV to immerse themselves, even if for only an hour, in a fantasy world where our rules don't apply and the impossible becomes possible?

Why is it that revolutionary and mind-bending movies like The Matrix resonate so fiercely with a global audience?

If you answered yes to these questions, admit it, there is a pull inside of you!

It is an inexplicable and unexpressed desire to be more than what you are currently. It is an urge to expand into greatness! It's a call to rise up to the impossible! It does not matter why you feel these stirrings within.

When you are prepared to follow these urges, to move out of a limited existence into a limitless life, you'll discover the reason. Meanwhile, there is something within you waiting to emerge!

There is a simple explanation as to why books and movies centred on superheroes with superpowers turn out to be astounding blockbusters. Films like The Avengers and The Matrix resonate so deeply because their themes of unlimited possibilities sing to something that lies sleeping inside each of you. They beckon to you, and stir a superpower inside of you that you've never known you possessed . . . and which you were never told about!

These movies are like a siren call, urging you to wake up from your deep sleep and break loose from your beliefs about limitation!

There is a profound sea-change in the air that is calling each and every one of us to wake up to what we feel is inside of us, deeply connected to something much bigger than you or I could imagine.

In this inner knowing is discovery, and access to the immense untapped potential of powers that are so astounding, that you'll manifest your greatest possibilities! You'll step into a new way of being!

Deep within you resides an inner knowing that there is more to you than the prosaic and mundane. You feel inside that you are meant to do more on this planet, to do more good, and to rise to higher purpose and leave behind a legacy that will benefit the world. There is a nagging inside of you. There is a yearning to do more and to be more. There is an inner desire to actualize more. You just don't know how . . . you've never been told!

18

It all starts to happen when you set free the abilities that you never even thought existed, and even more, that were always dormant within you.

I invite you to come down this rabbit hole with me!

Our entire world is focused around a programming of limitations, scarcity, and fear. It is only when you learn how to unplug from the matrix of fear, and learn how rewrite your programming, that your hidden potential starts to blossom.

Throughout this book, in every chapter, and on every page, I am not only going to expand your awareness into the realm of unlimited possibilities, I am going to take you on a journey to help shift you INTO the realm of unlimited possibilities!

You may have heard stories of people who were crippled but are now walking again without the help of a cane, or of tumours disappearing from someone's body, and you may have dismissed them as random miracles of faith that would never happen to you. You may have envied the person who found his or her soul-mate when all hope was gone, and you fear that you are doomed to a life of loneliness because you've had a string of unsuccessful relationships. You convince yourself that your soul-mate doesn't exist and you brace yourself to be alone, or you settle for less because you are afraid of loneliness.

Let me assure you that you can have your soul-mate, you can have your dream career, and you can have a whole lot more!

You are meant to have abundance with which to create and contribute to the world. You are meant to have energy to blaze new trails, and you're meant to have robust health!

There is another secret, which I will expand upon later, that has been misunderstood and it is that secret of connection that will truly set you free!

Think about it, you have been told that once you are sick, it's either a bunch of pills or it's the end of the road for you. You're programmed to believe that you must be a people pleaser, and to hang on to that job because it's a tough market out there, so don't rock the boat!

However, denying your soul-felt desires, suppressing your creative urges, or denying the urges to be more than you've ever imagined, just so that you fit in, manifests in a dis-ease like anxiety, depression, anger, and sadness.

Exposing yourself to unrelenting stress, anxiety, or sadness is not a natural part of modern society, no matter what you may have been told!

It's not meant to be part of any healthy society but we don't question if there are any alternatives. We buy into the programming that we've been subjected to from a very young age. What so many people never realize, is that your soul is here to love and be loved, and THAT is the true essence of who you are!

However, the fear is that if you wake up to the true power within, you will walk away from the world that has controlled you for so long, leaving everything that you know behind you.

It is crucial that you delete the programming that you have grown up with, and plug into new ones that are of service to you. It is necessary for you to re-examine the beliefs that have kept you unchanged and to remember who you truly are, and the abilities that you possess within. You are a superhuman, but if you cannot remember why you are here on this Earth School, life will stay the same. It'll be boring, it'll be beige, and it will be hard! It will be a winner-takes-all world and you'll be left behind . . . because that's what you've been told!

The only way to succeed is to get good grades, work hard at all costs, and don't buck the system!

Yes, I call this reality "Earth School." It's a place where we come to gain experiences.

To learn, to surpass our limitations, and to remember that we are all made of the same dust of which the planets and stars are made, and that we all carry within us a great creation energy waiting to be birthed!

By understanding the power of your body, and connecting to the messages it sends you, you can reshape your world instantly. Your brain is wired to keep you safe in this particular reality and to avoid risk by sticking to the conventional. You can harness that very same brain to rewrite old programming, to disentangle yourself from beliefs that no longer serve you, and to rebuild your foundation. It's for YOU to define what is true for you and what's not! Don't just buy into what your parents, family, and community believe!

The world runs on autopilot! When you turn the autopilot off, start to drive your own ship, and connect to a place bigger than yourself, true blessings and miracles are bound to unfold!

When Star Wars was first released, I was just six years old. There was so much electrified buzz about it and I was all excited to get to the movie. My dad whisked my sister and I off to the theatre and with our popcorn in hand, we settled in, ready for movie magic!

I had no idea that I would be glued to my seat, and that another kind of magic would unfurl for me. I had no clue that this diminutive, mystical, old green alien who spoke in cryptic sentences . . . Yoda . . . would change my world!

Trust me when I say that God works in mysterious ways!

Even as I write this, it is as if I am six again! Mesmerized by Yoda lifting the X-wing Starfighter out of the Dagobah swamp, using only his mental focus and a slight wave of his hand. Everything about that scene sang to me. I wanted to be Yoda! I wanted to do magical things and help people find their way to greatness! I wanted to learn about this great mystery of "the Force" so badly!

I would daydream trying to figure out the meaning of it all, but being so young I had no idea, I wouldn't figure it all out until much later in life.

My enthusiasm was dismissed as childish imaginings. "It's just a movie. It's make-believe. It's Hollywood, there is nothing real about it!" the detractors said, and there were many in number!

I was just a young and often sickly girl. Nonetheless, I wanted to believe with every fibre of my being, and every cell in my body, that I would be Yoda. That I would use my inner power and the force of the Universe to make a change in the world, and to make a difference wherever I went.

In the movie, Yoda got testy with Luke because in his eyes, Luke was gifted with the Force but couldn't overcome his disbelief because he had never done it before. Luke tried to lift the X-wing, but he couldn't succeed no matter how hard he tried.

"Clear your mind, clear your mind," Yoda admonished. Simple words, but they sank deep into my subconscious.

Luke resisted and kept rebutting Yoda. He said, "You want the impossible!" to which an exasperated Yoda replied, "That is why you fail!" and immediately showed Luke how to harness the Force.

You could hear a gasp of wonder from the audience during this spellbinding moment! Suddenly, on a big screen in a movie from

Hollywood, we were told that we could do wondrous things! That we could be more than this small, limited human that we always believed ourselves to be.

We could reach for the stars! We could tap into a boundless universal power called "the Force!"

In my youth I was bored with the school curriculum, hated memorization, and had poor grades. From my perspective as an adult, I can see that our current educational systems have taught us only to believe in the logical workings of our minds, while denying the urgings of our emotional intelligence or the soft guidance of our intuition.

But that's not who we really are!

We are not just a mind and we are not only wired to logic. We are feelings, and intuition, and Spirit!

Believing that only the mind is all powerful keeps us disconnected from the consciousness of a Universal Power, whether you call it God, Creator, or Divine Spirit.

What if you had been taught differently from a young age? What if you were taught from birth to access your feelings for answers, to make important decisions based on how you FEEL about this or that? To listen to the intuitive voice that is linked to the subconscious, which processes 400 billion bits of information per second, versus the 2,000 bits of information by the conscious, logical mind.

What if following your knowing was more important than memorizing dates and ancient history? What if learning to listen to the whispers of your body, and to the voice of an intelligence much bigger than you or me, was taught from birth? Imagine how life would be so different for everyone who exists on planet earth!

This is what connecting through your heart means. Your heart-drive, as I call it, is like the hard drive of your computer. If you take the hard drive out of your computer, it fails. If you remove your heart, you can no longer carry on.

This powerful muscle is the core of keeping each of us alive, but it is also the holder of all of the information connecting you to all of your desires. Reaching into the intelligence in the body and the heart allows you to tap into the energy of creation, but this is not an easy thing to do when the programming of the world is to rely on logic, rote work, and to believe only in what we can see. Relying only on your mind is a form of disempowerment. It's as if you are trying to row a boat without a paddle . . . and with only with one hand! It may get you somewhere, but it will be very slow, it will take much longer than necessary, and just as likely, you may be sailing around in circles!

Tapping into creation energy is like strapping on a rocket booster, it gets you from here to there at lightning speed! That's why miracle healings happen when patients tap into a power that supercharges them. The good news is that this power lies within you!

One of Yoda's most iconic lines is, "Do or do not. There is no try!"

In this reality, we are all stuck on trying because when faced with something we haven't encountered before, or which no one has achieved before, we don't believe that it is possible, so we "try" . . . instead of just doing!

We get trapped in our minds, and we tell ourselves, "I haven't heard of this before. It was not taught to me in school, so it cannot be true!"

This is where you get stuck—just because your logical brain cannot believe in a force greater than what logic dictates.

Doubt takes away from our abilities to self-actualize. It saps away our creative powers. It creates less, not more, for each of us. Without complete faith in the limitless, you give up . . . and you stay stuck in your brain.

You stop seeking! You ignore the miracles, and you question what you are feeling without paying heed to the important messaging that it is sending to you.

The Force that Yoda taps into is pure Divine energy, and it's by harnessing this energy within you that you achieve the impossible. Now think about it, it's pure power that lies untapped within you that no one wants you to let out, because it would scare many people to see how powerful you are!

When the movie was over, I played that scene over and over. I had every little toy from the show but Yoda was my hero!

However, on returning home after the movie was over, doubt crept in! My sicknesses were still with me and I still didn't feel safe in my environment. I was surrounded by angry adults, and I was still having breathing difficulties. The doubt grew and grew, sucking out my desire and my conviction that I could be a force like Yoda.

It was just a movie, everyone around me said, and they told me to get back to the grind of school, which I never liked. I had no inkling then, but my body was hanging onto the illnesses and going through many pains because it thoroughly rejected the flawed educational system. Even though I was so young, I knew that I was a misfit in that system, which bored me thoroughly and didn't spur nor inspire my imagination.

I suspect that many children reject school today because in their inner knowing, they know it's wrong to just feed a thinking mind and ignore the feeling heart.

I fought to hang on to my dream in the rude reality that I was in. Star Wars planted a seed in me that I watered and nurtured with love. It blossomed when I needed it most, to remind me of the power that I had inside.

Open New Doorways by Asking Why

For many years I asked, "WHY?"

If you picked up this book, you're probably the same as me. I questioned, I cajoled, I railed, and I shook my fist at the Universe!

Why do I need to go through this garbage in life?

Why can't life be easy and fun, like it is for everyone else?

Why me? Why me? Why me?

Sound familiar? If it does, let me assure you that I have been there and come out the other side and that I know, without a shred of doubt, that you can too!

You can change the way that you think about yourself and the world. You can self-heal, and you can tap into inner knowing—you can be more!

All of the experiences on Earth School are just that . . . EXPERIENCES! What you have come here to learn and to explore will shape what you will go through.

When the going got especially tough, I would find myself sitting on the end of my bed, railing at the Universe and yelling, "SERIOUSLY? Who in her right mind would choose this life of physical pain, depression, and anger? Are you insane?!"

I was furious! Why would I have willingly chosen so much anguish?

I was having a hard time understanding why I would opt for such stinging pain, prolonged agony, and untold anguish to unfold in my life. Why would anyone? Why did I have to live through so much struggle and strife? I stopped believing in a God or a Universal Creator because if there was Heaven, why did I pick Hell?

When I finally, consciously, started on my own journey at the age of 32, I increasingly gleaned what Earth School was all about. It was to teach us that we had FREE WILL to make CHOICES, and that the paths that we travel on are meant for us to learn to undo destructive patterns from a long time ago.

If not for those dark times, I would not have appreciated it as fully and as gratefully when life became easier. Now, I am grateful for all of the crap that I had to live through, because I couldn't have arrived at what I am doing today without having experienced pain and suffering.

My life was 95 percent crap, and now it is 95 percent amazing!

This is what doing the inner work is all about!

It helps you to navigate through those bumpy days with more ease and less torture. Just as importantly, you can shorten those testing days and get the lessons intrinsic to the experience in two days, rather than labour and languish for 2 years!

As you remove the old, self-limiting programs and make new heart-based choices, life magically changes!

What happens next?? New work shows up, along with new caring lovers, supportive friends, and money starts to flow. You become detached from the outcomes and you stay neutral to whatever will be. You stop controlling every detail of your life and the stress lifts off of the body!

In our current world, self-worth is measured by constantly accomplishing and accumulating. We buy more, we throw away more, we live in bigger houses with bigger environmental footprints, and we have expensive cars that we don't really need.

Consciously re-pattern your behaviour and beliefs in order to create the new grand life that awaits you when you begin this journey. Don't fall prey to unconscious patterns like stress eating, or stress shopping, or repeating life-diminishing choices like constantly falling for people who just can't commit, and inevitably break your heart.

Upend everything that you have been told, break free to new ways of thinking, and claim a new way of being. When you do that, you change your world!

We have been taught that we are limited and we are taught that our thoughts are limited. When you want to create a connection with the God Consciousness to change your life, you must unlearn all that you have learned.

Now this is a huge undertaking, because on any given day, at any given time, innumerable limiting beliefs will run through your mind. I call that the "enemy spirit."

It loves to rear its ugly head when you are on the verge of a breakthrough in life. It will plant seeds of doubt all of the time . . . so beware!

You may say to yourself that you are not good enough, pretty enough, tall enough, or handsome enough, or that you cannot do that because you do not know how. This list of limitations can go on and on, and unless you check it, it will keep replaying and it will exert a toll on you. The fears that you play over and over again in your mind will keep you stuck, and life will be as you've always known it. Your body will weaken and soon life loses its joy.

As I have discovered, when a limiting belief is ready to leave, you will feel unwell and your body will start to react. Many people will ignore the promptings until it is way too late, and then their next best step is to go and see a doctor.

I am not being anti-doctor here at all! However, the issue is that far too many people surrender their power over to their doctors, without fully understanding that their doctors work within their own set of limited beliefs!

Under today's medical system, doctors are still focusing on getting rid of the symptoms, rather than getting down to the root causes.

It is a time of integration, we can no longer support being separated from our bodies. This kind of separation will not work to your benefit for the next years of your life.

Thankfully, alternative modalities are being increasingly accepted, even if users of alternative remedies still remain amongst the minority.

When your illness is caused by emotions that have outstayed their visit in your body, it's time for you to get them out, and dissect any limiting beliefs that keep you in disempowerment. The body is like a magnificent computer and guide. Frustration, anger, anxiety, fear, or feeling of lack or insecurity—these are all signals from your body, screaming at you that something is wrong and that you should pay attention . . . because it's time to make necessary changes! When you have ignored an emotion for far too long, an illness will emerge. This is the only way the body knows that it will get your attention.

If you don't know where to start, the best point of origin is to explore viewpoints and ideas that appear revolutionary and unreal to you.

Put it this way, you are sick because of your current set of beliefs and ideas, so it stands to reason that you may be able to heal by subscribing to concepts previously foreign to you.

Seek out different avenues and make choices that make your body feel lighter and happier!

Staying connected to the energy of belief opens even more doorways to new possibilities that you once believed were outside of your capability. When you immerse yourself in reading the works of those who have broken free of limitations, when you stay receptive to stories of miracles rather than denying them, you are rewiring yourself.

You are creating a space, within and without, for more to come to you.

Claim back your power, and become the superhuman that you really are!

Limitation is just a skin that you wear, one enforced on you by old conditioning and outdated concepts. Limitless is your way forward!

Take the first step towards being limitless by removing the word "try" from your vocabulary and from your consciousness. There is only doing!

Even when you fall down, you keep going by putting one foot in front of the other.

Never give up and never limit yourself by believing that you can't. Imagine how different our modern lives would be if the Wright brothers had given up on their belief that man could fly. Just because we have never seen it, does not mean that it cannot happen! How do you think we got cell phones and computers? We got them because someone said, "I do not care what your limiting belief is, I am going to follow my vision and I am determined to keep going!"

Feel the exhilarating energy of the power of limitless, surging through your body as you read this—FEEL it—absorb it until all your cells are soaked in it!

I am reminded of the time that I worked in film and television. I was running a post-production house at that time and my friends, who were working on a set, asked me if I wanted to be an extra. I thought, "Why not!", it would be fun and I would have the chance to get out of the office. If you know anything about being an extra, you would know that you sit around a lot and do very little while you wait to be called. You have time to strike up conversations and get to know the people around you.

I was sitting next to this man who had the most unique face and he was exquisite at his craft. He was one of the principal actors, but he engaged with us, the extras, while he waited for his call. Although he was in his 80s, he had so much life to him!

I said to him, "You are incredible at acting! Have you done this your entire life?"

He looked at me with a charming smile on his face.

"Oh, no, far from it! I was bored and I always wanted to act, so I decided to get into it last year. I haven't stopped working since!"

I was awestruck that this man, now in his 80s, didn't let any of the obstacles—be it ageism or inexperience—keep him from going after his dream. He had proven to me that anything is possible!

Getting Started

How do you tap into your superhuman abilities? Here are some simple first steps:

1. Believe that this is the realm of unlimited possibilities. You can be a superhuman now! You don't have to wait 10 years.

2. Don't give up, EVER! When you are healing, you must be prepared to try everything, even a modality that seems absurd and silly to you. You must be willing to be a seeker and to keep looking.

3. Listen to your intuition! Don't second-guess it! Remember, it is your decision and you are the only one who can decide how to go ahead with restoring and regenerating your life. If you are working with someone who is unable to help you to release your issues . . . keep looking! Keep the clear intention that you'll find the right answers to heal you, as they are all within you. I did! . . . I found the answers because I never gave up the faith!

4. If you quit too early, you may miss out on the healing miracle that you need, because the miracle you are looking for may just be behind the next door you knock on.

5. Treat every step forward as a miracle. For many decades, getting out of bed was a miracle for me, and I was grateful for being able to accomplish even that.

6. Get comfortable with being uncomfortable! When you wander out of familiar territory you may be laughed at, you may be labelled as being ridiculous, or you may be bullied by peers, as I was when I was in school.

Wrapping up this chapter, let me segue into a short story here.

I wasn't born with eye teeth, so throughout grade school my mouth looked strange. That, combined with my uncontrollable body shakes, made me the victim of endless bullying.

Additionally, I didn't like school, I wanted to learn through play and inspiration. Instead, I felt like I had a ball and chain attached to my leg because my imagination just couldn't take flight. The result was that I was constantly told that I was dumb and that I was stupid.

I chose to ignore the scorn and the disbelief that coloured my years while growing up. I overcame any talk about being less-than and I healed myself after decades of being written off.

I believed that my body was powerful and that I was capable of self-healing.

It wasn't until my university days, when a professor had me take an IQ test and it showed that my scores were off the chart, that I fully understood that I wasn't dumb. I just learned differently than the system. I was able to see life from a new perspective.

I started to reclaim my power and realized that a grade from a teacher didn't define what I could and could not do in life!

I am smart, I am creative, and I am unlimited . . . and so are you!

Testimonial 2:
We Got Our Lives Back Thanks To Tracy

Hi Tracy,

It's Mat.

Thank you so much for your shout out the other day; you had us both crying with happiness and an immense feeling of love.

"Beth, my partner, and I started on Tracy L Clark's Miraculous Academy Partnership program some months back, and we have also completed two Body Regen Modules.

I cannot express enough in words what Tracy and her programs have done for me personally, but if I could sum it up, it would be that she has given me my life back. She has given me the wings to fly and, in turn, I now have the strength to start helping other people to find their wings and fly as well.

Tracy teaches you to firstly focus on yourself, and to release all the things that your body has held on to for so many years; and on top of that, to truly start loving yourself and putting yourself first, and feeling the love of God/the Universe flow through you. It is not possible to help others if you do not feel that love and have that love for yourself.

I personally experienced an extremely traumatic life changing experience as a 17-year-old boy—an act of terrorism which left me with eventually being diagnosed with PTSD. For nearly 30 years, I could not deal with the power my emotions had over me due to that event. It all came to a head 6 years ago, when I lost my dad to acute myeloid leukaemia; within a year, I tried to take my own life with the anti-depressants I was on. My second marriage had broken up, and I ended up living with my mum and could barely leave the house. Now, 6 years later, I am in a new relationship, with my soul mate, Beth. I am free of the anti-depressants, which I had been on for 20 years, and I am working in education, which was something that I was wanting to do for 20 years previously, but always came up with excuses why I couldn't! Tracy helped change all of that!

I am now working one on one with a selectively mute boy, who talks at home but not at school. I have been working with him since April. In the past couple of months, with Body Regen, Tracy worked on releasing the blockages and issues in him that were causing the selective mutism, and gave me (and all the group) the tools to keep releasing these issues. Within two weeks, I and his class teacher, and another child in the class, started a word game; in one 5-minute session, he spoke more words to me than he had in the previous 8 months. My heart literally melted, and I could barely hold back the tears of joy.

Tracy, through Body Regen, has also helped me to clear and deal with issues over being bullied as a child, which still has power over me, in not being able to speak up for myself and stand in the strength of my own truth. I now have found my voice and have felt the shackles release.

As I said at the beginning, Tracy has given me my wings and allowed me to help others find their wings.

I cannot ever thank you enough Tracy . . . and this is only the beginning!

Thank you, Tracy, and thank you, God x3, for coming into our lives.

Lots of Love,

Mat

Chapter 3

Piece by Piece, Step by Step,
From Agony to Joy

"The truth will set you free, but first it will piss you off . . . "

– Tracy L Clark

When the Universe smacks you on the side of the head, do you see that as a gift? Or do you get all worked up and upset, and rail at the skies and ask, "Why me?"

There is a common saying that when life gives you lemons, make lemonade, but what happens when the lemons themselves are bruised and rotten? What then?

For most of my life, I beat myself up. I perceived that everything that happened to me made me "less than," and that I would never become strong enough to be the woman that I longed to be.

Ever since I was born, all I knew was that I attracted bad things to me, and that I played the victim. I was so great at attracting the bad things, that I would imagine the worst-case scenario for everything, in the hope that something good would happen. I would call it reverse manifestation!

I was the queen in manifesting nasty experiences—trust me! I manifested people who took from me, stole from me, called me horrible names, and bullied me, even when I was an adult. Each time some ugly incident happened, I shrank inside and I felt smaller and more insignificant than before and effectively, I gave away more of my soul!

Since I only knew a world of bad news, what I was creating was from a perspective of bad news. I allowed life to continue to smack me on the side of the head every day with more crap. It was not until many years later that I understood what the lesson was and how I had it all backwards.

The Universe was serving me experiences, as painful or fearful as they were then, to get me to step into my greatness as a human being. It wanted me to stand up and say, "No More!"

The Universe was egging me on to stand up and boldly claim, "I matter! I have something special inside of me too!!!"

However, since I had no reference point of what represents a good life, I kept choosing what I knew even if it wasn't optimal, because it was safe!

Yes, it was safe because I knew it, I knew how to live and function in chaos. I lived in victim mode, physically and mentally, because that was the only programming that I knew from the friends and family around me.

One day I decided that I'd had enough, the life I was leading was no longer working!

Everyone gets that divine moment when realization hits you, and you fully grasp that something really has to change or it would be the end of you.

My divine moment happened with the birth of my second daughter, Christy.

After that, I caught on to a truth: Every experience that we go through is a gift from the Universe, no matter how much pain, anxiety, or fear we may be going through at that time. The other truth is that while the decision to change your life for the better can happen in a flash, putting into place the pieces of a new life, and the new steps that you have to take off of your beaten track, will take time and in the beginning, you may feel like crap!

You'll suffer fear of the unknown, fear of making the wrong moves, and you may fall prey to the seductive illusion that your old life was better because it was a known quality.

Let me encourage you to act in spite of the fear, despite the fear, and because of the fear! Grab the opportunity that comes your way, or better yet, create the opportunities to remake your life.

Don't let fear keep you stuck in your old ways! You only have one go around in this lifetime, so make it count! You will have to endure a little pain, but if you change your perspective and embrace the new, you are priming yourself for miracles!

Once I saw that the people who let me down or who hurt me were in fact returning a piece of me to myself, my life took a different turn. When I learned to forgive them, to bless them, to thank them, and in fact acknowledge them as gifts, I began to reclaim my power.

Yes, even the husband had who abandoned me while I was bleeding profusely in the surgery room during Christy's birth was a gift. This was the very same man who had refused to take care of our crying baby during the night because he was too tired to get up. I couldn't leave my baby crying distressingly for help. So in my severely weakened post-surgery state, still with fresh stitches, I hung on to the side of the mattress for stability as I lowered myself from the bed to the floor, and crawled on all fours to my daughter's crib to comfort her.

I endured so much pain that I cried myself to sleep, on the floor beside her crib.

Yes, that man was a gift because I woke up to appreciating that I deserved more and better. He taught me to find my voice and to say, "No more!" He taught me not to be afraid and to stop being a people pleaser. He taught me that I had more inside of me, more strength and more courage than I ever could have imagined!

This pain helped me to learn how to make powerful choices that were aligned with my soul. The greatest gift was when I stopped second-guessing my soul's desire and trusted the Universe to respond to me. It took me the better part of five years to create my new life, but first I had to endure the life-threatening agonies of my second pregnancy.

My Body Turned Black From Blocked Blood Flow

It was a very difficult pregnancy, complicated by a very rare and painful condition called venous engorgement, which happens when blood flow is obstructed. The inside of my groin swelled up to the size of two large bananas and the doctors initially thought that I had developed hernias.

When I finally got around to driving myself to a specialist, he took one look at me and pointed out that the swelling was in the veins, and that I needed to immediately consult with a vein specialist.

At this time, I could barely walk. It hurt to stand because the weight of the baby added extra pressure to the areas where I was feeling pain. When I heard his recommendation to consult with another doctor, I did not know whether to be relieved because it was a severe condition and therefore the pain was justified, or scared because I was barely mobile and didn't know if it was going to get far worse.

By the time I had consulted the specialist in venous disorders my body had turned black and blue. From under my breastbone to my ankles, the obstructed veins had twisted and had become so gnarled that it looked like I had bunches of grapes hanging off of my body.

I would wear long dresses to hide my disfigurement but I couldn't hide the tears caused by the pain and the stress of toughing out an agonizing pregnancy.

I also had to endure the difficulties of simply standing up while looking after my three-year old at home, who wanted to play and be fed.

I didn't have family around me to help and I ended up going on long-term disability from work. Unfortunately, my husband at the time offered little help. He had a hard time managing his own life, and as such, he would take on little tasks only when it suited him. He wasn't working at that time but was pursuing ideas of what he wanted to achieve with all of the free time on his hands. The end result was that for many nights I would lie in bed crying.

All I needed was someone to show me some care! Someone who would make me dinner, or rub my aching back, and basically, just take care of me.

At that time, I was afraid to speak up or to ask for something that I needed. I shied away from confrontation, so I didn't speak up. My husband had a bad temper and I felt as if I was walking on egg shells every moment of the day.

I had to drive myself to the hospital for frequent check-ups to ensure that I wasn't developing blood clots. The doctor and the medical staff would often query if I was a single mother because I turned up at the appointments alone, without anyone giving me a hand, even though I couldn't stand up for more than five minutes at a time.

I didn't bring this up to my husband. I became accustomed to putting on different masks to hide my emotions, even though I felt like I had reached the end of my rope on countless occasions.

It was my eldest daughter Nina who kept me going. She had so much light in her! She was always singing, dancing, and laughing and I knew that I could not let her down.

One hot summer day, we went to the grocery store together and I decided to wear shorts. At the checkout, a lady behind me spoke out loudly to her mother, "Oh, my God. Look at her legs!"

Back in our car, I had a breakdown and cried uncontrollably for 30 minutes. I felt so alone and weighed down by the burdens of my health and a difficult pregnancy, and my three-year-old daughter kept assuring me that "It will be okay Mommy!"

She came to appointments with me, all excited that she was going to be a big sister. She was the only joy in my world at that time. She kept me going every day with her smile, her singing, and her dancing. She offered me some consolation, but I was ridden with guilt. How did I end up in a marriage with such an uncaring partner?

How could I explain to my daughter that her father felt that he had far more important things to do than to take care of his terribly sick and very pregnant wife?

It became a very lonely journey but the worst was yet to come!

After my final appointment with my doctor, they informed me that I urgently needed to get to the hospital for an emergency C-section. As they were prepping me and wheeling me into the surgery room, the only thought going through me was "Get this kid out and let me die!"

I was drowning in an avalanche of unhappy emotions, feeling so alone and unwanted, not having a clue as to where I belonged or why I was even in this battered life. I was gripped by an insane fear!

I was no stranger to fear, having been kidnapped at the age of five, but this time the fear that gripped me was different. My heart was pounding and racing!

Meanwhile, the attending doctor was hurrying everyone to get the baby out as soon as possible because so much blood had collected in my body.

The enormity of everything became too overwhelming, and I started to pass out.

When they made a cut for the C-section, the pooled blood that had been dammed up in my body spurted out everywhere—onto the floor, the operating table, the walls, and even the ceiling—as if we were in a B-movie horror film.

I so badly wanted to close my eyes and give in to checking out of this life and not come back. I was done on so many levels, and I wanted nothing at all to do with this baby . . . or my life!

This had not been a joyous pregnancy, it was rife with pain and agony.

I had a near death experience when I was seven and I could still recall what it felt like on the other side. I kept wandering in and out of wanting to leave.

If there was one thing that kept pulling me back, it was the anaesthesiologist, who was the earth angel that came to my aid. He kept saying, "Tracy, stay with me! I am going to give you some more medicine for pain relief. Look at me, stay with me!"

I retorted, "NO, I want to go!" but he took hold of my will and urged me to stay. "You are going to be okay!" he insisted. He anchored me to this dimension because the temptation to leave was almost overpowering. When my baby girl Christy screamed, I switched my focus back to this body and I voluntarily stayed.

When it was all over and they had stitched me up, I opened my eyes and was shocked to see blood-soaked towels everywhere. It was unfathomable that so much blood had gushed out of my body!

The nurses took my baby away, and my husband was nowhere to be found. Once again, I was alone!

In recovery, I couldn't move because my body had been numbed by the anaesthetic, I could only shake my head. My mind was clouded by painkillers and I was still out of it. I kept asking the nurses where I was and how I could get out.

I was exhausted and traumatized. The nurses soon came to get me to take me to my bed upstairs. They were cold and uncaring, and they moved me so quickly through the corridors that I was going to throw up. I told them this and they ignored me three times!

Of course, to their horror, I threw up everywhere! It wasn't as if I hadn't given them fair warning but they acted as if they had no inkling of my nausea. It's fair to say that I was pretty miffed at that point in time. Why wasn't anyone listening to me? Why were they ignoring me?

I finally settled in, and I was still alone! Eventually, my husband showed up.

He said that he had left the hospital because he was afraid that I was going to die. I had no answer to that, I was the one who was possibly dying and he left because he couldn't handle it?

That night, I cried myself to sleep but was woken up by involuntary body trembles. I was shaking all over and gasping for breath, like a fish out of water. I still couldn't move, nor could I feel any sensation from the neck down.

Thankfully, I managed to reach the distress button. When the nurse finally came, she pulled back the sheets to see blood everywhere on the bed. I had haemorrhaged so much, that I had no iron left in my body and I couldn't keep myself warm.

They cleaned me up and when the morning nurse came around, she asked me if I was a single parent. Once again, the issue that I was alone loomed over me. It was not surprising that they thought that I was single because my husband was barely around, and definitely not during the crucial life and death moments.

The nurses told me that I couldn't be discharged unless there was someone at home to take care of me. They had somehow sensed that the "barely there" husband would not amount to much help. Maybe it was a premonition of things to come!

Thankfully, my mom was coming and they waited for her to arrive before officially discharging me.

I was on bed rest for a long time in order to heal and to regain the strength to walk. My mom had begged me to leave my husband, and to go home with her, as I was always on edge and uptight in my home environment.

The people that knew me well, understood that my head would shake when I was under severe stress. At this point, I was under such acute stress that my head would shake so hard, that it appeared as though I was having seizures.

Shortly after we had returned from the hospital, my older daughter spilled milk all over the living room. In my rush to clean up the mess, so that my husband would not freak out about it on his return, I almost ripped open my stitches from the delivery.

My mom witnessed everything and she begged me to leave with her! How was I going to take care of my two girls after she left? I couldn't count on any kind of support from my husband in any way at all!

Many mothers suffer postpartum depression but I was assailed by it even more than most. I became more depressed, I was angry with my current lot in life, and I was also deeply saddened. I was lost, how did I even end up here? What choices had I made that led me to this?

My daughter's birth should have been a celebratory event. Instead, I felt punishing shame, extreme loneliness, and crushing guilt that I wasn't immediately bonding with my child. I actually wanted nothing to do with her for six long months because I was so fatigued and worn out, that I had nothing left of myself to give.

Yet, eventually, it would be my two daughters, Nina and Christy, that gave me the strength to leave my marriage, take back my power to choose the shape that my future would take, and activate my will and my life force to create the life that I now have.

From the Jesus Moment to a New Life

My youngest daughter's birth, and what came after, was my "come to Jesus" moment—that pivotal point where I stood up to my fears and staked a claim for a richer and more fulfilling life. I was determined to move away from pain and hopelessness, from a loveless marriage and a lack of self-love, to a life where I celebrated my self-worth and could be of service to others.

The Hand of God moves in mysterious ways, and it took me five years from this point of recognition to finally getting out of my marriage.

During those years I enrolled in self-help classes because I perceived that I was the problem. I was overly sensitive, and I gave in to overthinking and overanalysing.

It painfully occurred to me that there were very few happy moments in my life.

I was shaped to believe that life was all about pain and suffering and little else.

As my body healed and I regained my strength, I forced myself to go back to work to support my family. For reasons known only to him, my girls' father had a very tough time working and it took him a while to find a job.

We lost many friends during those years because my husband didn't enjoy having visitors over. My world was centred on my kids and my work.

During those years, I made a plan to save for a future for what remained of our family—my two girls and myself.

I became more distant from my husband. Although I kept most of my feelings to myself, which was how I was brought up, I was increasingly fired up by anger. Sex was not motivated by a desire for connection, it was an act to discharge anger. When he was sick, I couldn't bring myself to take care for him.

Looking back, I don't think that my husband didn't love me, he just didn't know how to love a person . . . and that was sad! He tried in the best way that he could but he didn't question, or seek to improve himself.

Meanwhile, I prayed for answers . . . but few came. My soul felt as though it had been abandoned in darkness. If there really was a God, why did the Creator put me through such hellish tortures? Sometimes God provided me with an opening.

We went to seek advice on our marriage and the counsellor asked to see me alone for a session. He pointedly told me to my face, "I wish your husband would hit you with a bat . . . because then you would leave!"

He continued, "You would be better off with a dog after you leave this marriage." I was astounded and I immediately rose to my own defence. I said, "I am not crazy!" but he persisted, "You are beyond neglected and your husband will never see that!"

I had no boundaries and I wanted love so badly, that I had trained him how to love me. The only way that I knew how to be loved was by neglect. That was my program from a very early age, and I played it out very well!

Those were harsh words but I felt the presence of an angel during that encounter. He was the first stranger who spoke directly to what was wrong with my life. The counsellor helped me to realize that a pattern of abuse by men ran in my family.

My dad couldn't cope emotionally with my mother, and my grandparents on my mother's side knew little but anger in their relationship. That was the normal I grew up with but now that I recognized what I had unconsciously manifested, I understood that I didn't have to put up with any more of it. In time, I found the courage to take the next critical steps for my own life.

When the opportunity finally came, I was ready to break free because during those five years, as hard as they may have seemed, I was dismantling those pieces of myself that had been shaped by what the world had told me that I should be. When I listened to my heart, I was slowly creating the me that I really needed to be, from the inside out.

By paying attention to my inner urgings and being mindful of each and every decision that I made, I was paving my way out of unhappiness to a joyful life.

Even when my path was clear, there were still hiccups. I had attempted to leave my marriage once before. My husband insisted that since I was the one working, I needed to pay him spousal support. It befuddled me that this well-educated man would be on the dole and expected his wife to support him.

Everything became nasty! My kids were then two and five years of age, and I figured that it would be best to calm the situation and batten down the hatches for an eventual move.

It was interesting to me that the fault was always mine, and that I was the one that needed to change, not him.

We proved right the wisdom that when couples don't grow together, when two people don't keep apace with each other's personal development, they would inevitably break away from each other's orbit and go their separate ways.

Eventually, the time did come and I broke free.

I'll continue with that story in the next chapter. Just to give you a little peek, they say that what happens in Las Vegas stays in Las Vegas. However, what happened in Las Vegas came back with me . . . and I found my wings to break free!

This is Not a Pity Party

I have had more than my fair share of trials and tribulations but at this stage of my life, I am now able to thank everyone who brought something into my life. With each encounter, they gifted me with a piece of myself—not the small, scared self who only saw abuse and pain, but the bigger self—who I found and reclaimed out of the ashes of painful experiences.

By blessing everyone who has gone through my life, broken relationships have been mended, love has returned to grace our lives, and we make joyous memories of an extraordinary life every day!

I have even blessed the Catholic school kids who threw rocks at me and screamed horrible things at me to scare me off when I was a child. Being as frail as I was, I couldn't fight back. Instead, I ran and hid behind houses and like any young kid, I failed to understand why I was being so horridly bullied. Now I know!

If you are reading this book, you are ready for a change!

Trust that the Hand of God is reaching out to you through these words, to awaken your sleeping self, to inspire you to make choices that serve you . . . not decisions that hurt you . . . and to treat each experience as a gift!

The message that God wants to deliver here is that you are all beautiful and Divine!

You have free will to take charge of your life, to ignite it with spiritual power and courage, and fill it with purpose. Your life is yours to sculpt! Don't let it be moulded by default, by the opinions of others, by the expectations of society that you don't want to measure up to, or by the programming with which you have grown up.

If you believe in a greater destiny for yourself, go all out for it!

You are not crazy to expect more and better, even if everyone around you is consumed with despair and hate. You are not the stories that you have been told!

You have to march to the beat of your own drum!

If people that you know don't change, it's because they are either not ready for it, or they are too afraid to take the plunge into the unknown.

However, just know that when you are ready to transform and to be of service to the world, the Universe reaches out to catch you when you make the jump, and it lifts you up to elevations that you never knew existed!

Question everything!!

Especially the beliefs that make you feel as if you are a square peg in a round hole.

When you are young, you may not know any differently because you listen to what your parents tell you, what your schoolteachers instil in you, and what religious groups and elders insist that you must do.

Most of us unwittingly become by-products of our family's patterning. They imprint on us the way we act and behave because while we don't really know it, we are taking on the emotions and feelings of our parents from the moment that we are born.

The environment in which you grow up greatly affects how you perceive your life, your successes, and your purpose.

Understand that leaving the old behind is not a failure! Failure is actually not daring to leave behind what no longer serves you.

For me, had I stuck to what was familiar, I would have remained angry and depressed, wrapped up in physical agony and pain, and I would never have found the strength to carry out my life's purpose. Had I not awakened, I would be dead today!

I am here to tell you that you can change old, outdated, patterning like a snake moults old skin, and create for yourself an extraordinary life.

I did . . . despite every hurdle, every physical difficulty and pain, and despite all of the emotional despair and abuse!

I thank God for YOU! . . . and for giving you hope that there's brilliant, glorious, and loving light at the end of your tunnel!

I thank God for giving you the courage to unlearn all that you've unconsciously absorbed and been programmed by. You are now able to remove conflict from your life and connect with the world at large as you've never done before.

I encourage you to thank God for all the joys that you have in your life right now!

My steepest hurdles have been my biggest blessings and I thank God for all of them!

You too can turn your worst pains into your deepest joys.

The moment you believe in this, is the moment you begin your transformation!

Testimonial 3:
Tearing With Joy And A Heart Full Of Love!

My dearest Tracy

THANK YOU!!! I am writing this email the evening of the completion of the 1st day of today's workshop. I have just taken my salt bath, sitting and recounting the events of today. I can't thank you enough for pushing me, making me feel vulnerable in front of a big audience today - thank you for choosing ME! I realized that my whole life I was never accepted by those around me so I fabricated this person that wanted to please everyone. I have continued that facade until I met you and joined TLC. Thank you

for making me understand that I can be the REAL ME, that person who loves people, who is caring, who loves GOD, who is empathetic to others, who has a voice, who wants to live by her TRUTH. I have always had criticism from childhood into marriage that when I show those beautiful qualities, they shun me, criticize with jokes and demean me. Today you made me realize that this community loves and doesn't judge and I am so grateful to have experienced that love today. I lost my voice again today, I physically at one point could not talk and I didn't like the feeling. I choose to push forward and leave the fear behind.

I had a talk with GOD during my bath. I told him all my desires - huge big dreams! It is the first time that I was able to formulate the things that I wanted. I have never been able to do that so this is a huge massive step for me. And I also understood why I wanted all those things I desire not just for me but for hopefully many others. AND I asked for the easy way!

I started on a journey of self growth and realization over 30 years ago, learning, reading, doing courses and workshops, different therapies and modalities and meeting different teachers along the way. I thank them all for their participation and contribution in my growth and placing me where I am today. YOU, however, have been the most impactful in the shortest time. You, my dear Tracy, continue to trigger me, push me, teach me, making everything easy to understand and learn. The work is on me, I know that. It's all up to me. But I also know that I have YOU, the evolutionary group of beautiful souls and the rest of the TLC community to support me, guide me, counsel me, accept me, praise me and love me in a way that I have never experienced. That was evident today. Thank you for this and thank you for the biggest gift, sharing your love!

I look forward to Day 2 of this amazing workshop!

In complete gratitude to you

Tearing with joy and a heart full of love!

AnnaMarie

xoxoxo

Chapter 4

It Started in Las Vegas;
I Believed and I Received

*"Open your eyes today to be in the wonder of
what the world is offering you."*

– Tracy L Clark

I have said this before and it may sound preposterous to many of you: Those who hurt us the most are our best gifts and our greatest blessings—but that doesn't mean we have to stick around them!

When a relationship is lacking in love, is filled with emotional abuse and is painfully dysfunctional, the greatest learnings come when we find the courage to leave. When we have the courage to believe that we deserve better!

The day to leave my husband finally came.

It was a cold, dark, snowy night. I know, many novels begin that way, and the new chapter in my life started that way—on a freezing night, deprived of warmth and light.

We were driving to celebrate Thanksgiving at my parents' home and the kids were sitting in the back of the car. My husband had never liked my family, and they didn't they like him either. Each time we visited them, I felt pulled in multiple directions. The arguments would start days before we visited my family. Whose side was I to take?

Looking back, I believe that my parents felt helpless in the face of my unhappy marriage. They didn't want to interfere, and they didn't know how, or what to do, to help me.

Inexplicably, during the drive my husband became very angry. He got so angry that the veins were popping out of his head, which I had seen many times as he would often fly into these rages of anger.

In that moment, something inside of me snapped and I kicked him out of the truck that I was driving. I locked him out and drove away. To my despair, our kids were crying and screaming in the back.

Eventually, I did turn around to go back and get him, and we stopped for a night at a hotel to gather ourselves.

It was complete chaos! I was tired of being the one who always had to accommodate another person's behaviour—the one who had to change, the one who had to be the good time, the one who had to tend to what everyone else needed— while I was dying inside, tasting the bitter ashes of my dead, unfulfilled dreams.

My husband had not changed since I married him, but I had, and therein lied the problem! He was still the man that I had married and the man that I called into my life. I was faulting him for being the same person he was when we met.

That, I would learn later, was not fair. He showed up exactly how I called him in to show up. However, I had changed because I had worked on myself. I had grown and was desiring and demanding to be treated differently.

Everyone has their demons and as I worked on mine, he remained the same, attached to his. We grew further and further apart as a result.

The events of the evening took place a year after I had set out on the path of digging deep within, to understand my source of unhappiness and the origin of my pain. I had made the choice to change; he stayed the same.

This is normal for many couples: one grows; the other stagnates.

How many times have you blamed those closest to you for not giving you what you require? . . . when the plain truth is that you changed and they never did.

What happens next is that you expect more and more as you grow more and more, and they give you less and less. The result is that you dwell in the pain of not being understood and not being fulfilled.

My parents knew something was up, since the town in which we overnighted was only a scant hour away from their home.

We were upset and distraught, and I certainly did not want to get to their house in that state. I collected myself and by the time we arrived I was calmer and much more together.

My mom suspected something was up but I didn't want to speak about it. Deep inside, I knew that I was done!

Physically, I was so worn out and anorexic that you could see my hip bones jutting out, and the contours of my ribs were pressing against my torso. My stomach was still irritated, I was still coping with nerve damage, and I was depressed. My doctors were worried about me, and they were managing me as well as they could, but it didn't seem that they could do much more for me. My body was failing again because my emotions were literally fried, thereby "frying" my internal organs.

This marked a significant turning point for me! A new pathway, and a new choice, would soon open up.

Two weeks later, I left for a girls' trip to Las Vegas with my mom, my grandmother, and my sister. It had been planned for some time, and feeling as worn out as I did, I was reluctant to go. I had never been to Las Vegas and because it was already paid for and booked, and I didn't want to be without my family, I forced myself to pack.

My grandmother and mother loved Las Vegas! They loved the entertainment, the neon lights, the sights . . . and yes, they were looking forward to a little gambling! I had never been on a girls' trip . . . so why not!

I remember that when I boarded the plane I was feeling very down. I was depressed and all I wanted to do was to drink myself into numbness so that I didn't have to deal with the mess that was my marriage, and the mess that was my body. Drinking was a big way to escape the pain that was pressing down on me, and many of you know exactly what I mean!

Have you arrived at that point in your life when you issue an ultimatum to God because you have nothing else? I was at that very point, and I clearly recall being on the plane and pleading with the Universe.

I said to myself, "I don't believe there is anything out there, no higher power, or no God. No one has to walk through this much pain if there is a Greater Being out there! However, I am on my hands and knees because I have nothing left and nowhere to turn. If there is something of a higher order, I need to know something. I need to know that there are good men out there. Good caring men! I need a sign, I cannot do this by myself anymore. I am DONE! It's time to change!" . . . and I left it at that.

When my sister and I arrived, we met up with our mother and grandmother at the hotel. We had arrived on Halloween, so you can imagine the colours, the frivolities, the music, and the sounds of people having a good time!

Based on what I was witnessing, it dawned on me that I had lived a very sheltered life. I had no words to describe what I saw before me but I was clearly intrigued that this was how many others lived!

We puttered around for a bit but because I was so worn out, we decided on an early night. My body was exhausted but my mind was roiling. Like a stormy day at the beach, waves of emotions would crash down on my consciousness with great frenzy and then retreat, only for another giant wave to beat down on me.

I felt that I couldn't get a breather. I had been pummelled throughout life by one giant wave after another but because I was so depleted, I stopped fighting.

I didn't know it that evening but my hurried prayer, born out of a desperate need, had been heard!

Trust and Follow the Signs

Some compassionate and loving Force had heard me and would orchestrate a series of events that evening to show me that my plea had been heard and answered.

I would like to add at this point that throughout our lives, many of us ask for signs to confirm that we've made the right decision, or thrown in our lot with the right person, or made the right turn in our life's journey.

Often we are blind to the signs that appear . . . or we overlook them!

We stay focused on the drama and keep looking for what we think is right for us now, rather than what Spirit has placed in front of us to grasp.

Maybe we expect a huge thunderbolt or a flash of lightning as a sign, but the Universe is gentle and sometimes the messages of hope are delivered in the form of the softest of whispers.

While growing up, we are not taught how to listen to the soft urgings of our bodies, or to the kind voices of our intuition. We've only been taught to make our choices and decisions based on rationality, logic, and what we can see, not what we feel.

If we had been schooled or encouraged differently at a young age to pay heed to our inner wisdom, all of our lives would be far richer, far more fulfilling, and filled with more pleasure and ease.

Pay close attention to what feels good and what doesn't.

Notice your energy levels—what uplifts you and what doesn't?

Above all . . . ASK!!! When you believe, you'll receive!

There were no signs when we got up the next morning and we did what we set out to do. We walked, window-shopped, walked, shopped, stopped for food and drink, and walked some more. I was still in a dark space and being surrounded by family who loved me, and having fun in a non-taxing way, worked out very well for me.

That night we dressed up for a concert. We were off to see Rick Springfield. I know that I am dating myself, but he was every girl's heartthrob when I was young. It was such a treat to see him perform live. My mom and grandmother were having the time of their lives, observing the people and the colour around them.

As we walked through the casino, my mother pointed to the men looking at us and made a joke about how oblivious my sister and I were to their stares. She said to me, "Don't you see the men looking at you like flies to a fly strip?"

I laughed and told her that she was crazy. Yet, without sounding egocentric, this has been a theme throughout my life. I am unaware of people or men checking me out, and I basically don't care! I stay within my bubble, which protects me.

Many people don't understand this, but that is the way it is with me.

After the concert, we walked past Studio 54. I had always dreamed of dancing at Studio 54 but I was the "good" girl who never stepped out of line, so clubbing that night was not on my radar. You could imagine how I was initially reluctant to enter a nightclub, but our mother enthusiastically encouraged both my sister and I to have a spot of fun.

We decided, "Why not!" and we said to each other, "Let's go! The worst thing that could happen is that we go home early!"

It was loud, colourful, and highly energetic! Women were hanging from the ceiling, dancing, twirling, and contorting in acrobatics. As a dancer, I found the entertainment fascinating!

It got me dreaming of what my life would have looked like had I not taken the safe path, and instead, followed my dreams.

I could have had a life filled with the joy of dancing. Watching the Las Vegas dancers stirred my deeply buried dream to be a dancer, a dream that I thought had actually died a long time ago.

A fireman immediately hit on my sister and would not leave us alone, even when we walked up to the second level to watch the club performers. I have nothing against firemen, my stepfather was one, but this man came across as being extra needy.

Eventually, my sister dodged the conversation by leaving to use the bathroom and even though she said that she would be right back, she did not return. I was peeved that she had left me alone with this man and I finally told him that I had to go and find her.

As I walked downstairs, I almost bumped into a performer holding a big snake. Snakes and I don't get along at all and the encounter made me all edgy and nervous!

Finally, I found my sister and noticed that she was having a conversation with a very handsome man.

I said to myself, "You bag! You leave me alone upstairs and you find yourself this handsome guy!" By that time, I had a few drinks in me and I was starting to warm up to the club atmosphere.

I was feeling free of the burden of all the roles that I played in life— loving mother, creative entrepreneur, and unhappy wife!

I mustered up the energy to confront both of them. As I walked over to my sister, this gorgeous man turned around, looked at me, and said, "Finally! You must be the most oblivious woman I've ever met. I thought that if I snagged your friend, you would eventually come downstairs."

I was floored! I was flabbergasted that this gorgeous man wanted to speak to me! He made an effort to meet ME?

It turned out that his name was Steve and he was visiting from New York City. It so happened that he was at the club for a bachelor's party. Steve and I hit it off immediately!

We danced and laughed all night, till 6 a.m. Yes, till the early morning hour of 6am!

Finally, we realized that the day was dawning and we had to get back to our respective hotels. We exchanged numbers, arranged to meet up later that evening, and off we went.

As my sister and I approached our rooms, we were a little concerned that our mom and grandmother had stayed up all night worrying about us. We opened the door with as much care as we could and there they were, up and dressed, and ready for the day. They didn't ask us a whole lot of questions, they were just happy that we were back and safe.

My sister and I changed and readied ourselves for another day out with family.

As I walked with my grandmother, she said that she wasn't at all worried about us but my mom had been. Yet when I spoke to my mom, she claimed that it was my grandmother who was fussing about us. No harm had come to either of us but it was still heart-warming to know that these two lovely women were concerned about my sister and I, even if we were adults.

When we sat down for a drink, my grandmother quizzed me. Whom did I meet? . . . and who was making me smile the way that I was?

It had been such a long time since she had seen such a happy expression on my face. I told her about Steve and also explained that even though Steve kept asking what my backstory was, I didn't want to say too much. I kept telling him throughout the evening that I did not care to talk about my life.

By this time, I was not wearing my wedding ring and the stress in my life was so high that some people thought that I was anorexic. Even my husband at the time believed me to be anorexic. I had lost so much weight that keeping a ring on my finger was not an option.

My grandmother bought me another drink and looked me straight in the eye. I will never forget the expression on her face when she said, "Tracy, do not make the same mistakes that I did, it's not worth it! Life is too short to spend it being miserable. I stayed for all of the wrong reasons and have endured much pain in my relationships. I have never seen you smile like you have today. You have your entire life ahead of you. It is your choice, so remember that!"

I listened carefully as she continued because it wasn't often that the women in our family would speak out about marital issues.

"Do what you need to do to get out because in the end, you cannot change him. You'll die if you stay in your marriage!" she insisted.

I wasn't extremely close to my grandmother but I will tell you that I heard the message loudly and clearly. I took it as a sign from the Universe, so trust me when I say that I have never forgotten that conversation to this day. I took her advice seriously because I knew that her marriage was like mine. It was abusive and she wasn't at all happy. To hear her speak so fervently about leaving an unhappy marriage sounded to me like a clarion call from the heavens.

Steve called later that night and asked to meet us at another club. Once again, I had so much fun dancing and laughing!

Sometime during the night, I had an epiphany. I realized that what I had asked for—a fun, kind, and caring man— was right in front of me!

The heavens had heard me and sent Steve my way!

We partied all night and yes, we had too much to drink—so much so, that we lost our way in the Bellagio casino. We were running around laughing out loud and having such a fun time, and we couldn't figure out how to get out of the hotel.

I was laughing!! I could not remember a time when I had laughed, but that didn't matter because we were having so much fun together!

Finally, we made it out the front door of the Bellagio. He grabbed hold of me, swung me around, and lifted me onto the ledge.

At that very moment, the Bellagio water show started.

The fountain lights were turned on, the music started, and water from more than a thousand fountains shot up into the air . . . some reaching as high as 460 feet!

Everything had been so well orchestrated that I felt as though I were in a scene from the movies, and even in my most feverish dreams I couldn't have imagined something as beautiful, as magical, and as wondrous, happening to me!

Steve kept asking about my story and once again, I answered that I couldn't talk about it.

We continued spending time with each other and we ended up at his hotel.

Don't get too excited! I wish I could say that we had memorable, wild sex, but that wasn't the purpose of our chance encounter. Steve behaved like a true gentleman and when I said that I had to leave, he walked me to the elevator.

He asked if he could see me again. I said, "I know why I met you and I thank you! . . . but we may not see each other again." He was a little confused and asked, "What do you mean? Why can't I see you again?"

He was still holding my hand as the elevator doors closed on us. As our hands parted, it was as if time stood still.

I walked back to my hotel with a dance in my step. My mom noticed how happy I was and said, "I don't know what happened, but I haven't seen you smile like this in many, many years!"

Steve was the answer to the prayer that I had muttered under my breath on the plane. God showed me that there were kind and caring men out there in the world.

It wasn't as if I wanted to bounce from a loveless marriage into the arms of another man . . . as cute, gorgeous, and fun as he was!

I did know that the Divine did care!

It was up to me from that point on to make deliberate choices that would make me happy. Many people in unhappy relationships look for someone to rescue them. They look outside of themselves, rather than looking to their own inner strength.

That is why many of you make poor choices!

I understood deep down that Steve was the push, the nudge from the Universe that I had to do this by myself, that I had to rescue myself!

However, the kindness that he showed me was beyond anything that I had experienced. My encounter with him was the answer to my prayers!

The Universe had heard my cries and had answered. It was now left up to me to take the next steps to move from a life ridden with fear, to one of complete understanding, total acceptance, and unconditional love.

I walked into my home late at night from the airplane ride. I did not go to the bedroom that I shared with my husband. I walked into the children's room and slept with my girls.

My husband walked in the next day and said to me, "It's over, isn't it? I should have gone with you to Vegas, I knew it! You've met someone!"

I looked at him calmly and said, "Yes, it is over!"

He was furious and he completely missed the point. It wasn't the man that I had met in Las Vegas that had changed our marriage, it was simply that I was done!

Nothing could save our marriage. I longed for more in my life.

I longed to figure out who I was, why I was here, and what purpose I had to fulfil.

Once my decision was made to end our marriage, I gave myself permission to dream again. You are probably wondering if Steve ever reached out to me. Yes, he did . . . a few times, but that's as far as it went. I thanked him for showing up in my world.

I knew that it was my time, time for a new chapter to begin!

I understood that the path ahead, over the next few years, would not necessarily be filled with ease and grace. I had to uncouple myself from much of what I had created, but I sensed that my life would be more peaceful.

When you make a deliberate choice to take a new, more personally fulfilling path, stay aware that it's not going to be roses and rainbows the next day!

However, when you are ready to do something different in your life, you open an energy doorway for God to do something different in your life as well!

In the movies, life is magically different the next day. However, it doesn't work that way, you need to put in the hard work!

You now need to build a new foundation, just like renovating your house. Sometimes the entire house has to come down and a new foundation must be built, so that the house can be strong and sturdy. When you build the new house, you will change the rooms and add new features that you never had before.

Your life is the same way, as you change the foundation of your life, all of the areas of your life will change with you. You have got to find the courage to walk down new roads and new paths that you would have never considered before. When you truly open to what shows up, miracles spring forth!

Just like the new house, your life will show up with new blessings, and new rooms filled with opportunities that you have always dreamed of because you told Spirit that you are ready!

With the new road now in front of me, I was reborn!

Testimonial 4:
Abundance Of Peace And Love In My Life!

Since joining the Evolutionary Academy I have experienced incredible transformational growth in all areas of my life. In less than a month of working with Tracy, I have been able to overcome many of the restrictions, blockages and fears that have prevented me in the past from living the life I've always dreamt of. Tracy is by far one of the most extraordinary people I have ever had the pleasure of meeting and working with. Within a short period of time working with Tracy and the Evolutionary Academy, I have seen my relationships grow stronger and now overflow with more love than ever before. I have also become more grounded and connected in mind, body and spirit, providing me with an abundance of peace and love in my life that I never thought possible. Prior to joining the Evolutionary Academy, I made decision-making harder than it needed to be. I tended to over think everything, become exhausted and overwhelmed. By learning to release fears and trust my heart, I am now able to let go of attachments to outcomes and make decisions with ease and grace. I am forever grateful for the life changing opportunities that are now present in my life thanks to Tracy and the work associated with the Evolutionary Academy!

Cheers,

Mike Awde

Chapter 5

The Mind is a Virus!

"The difficulties are not meant to defeat you, they are meant to promote you. Don't give up! You're about to be promoted!!"

– Tracy L Clark

The mind is a wonderful and powerful thing!

It takes us on flights of imagination, to help us create the next best thing that moves humanity forward. It is able to make order out of chaos, and finds the beauty in the noise. It's able to make sense of music and math, and to tell the difference between the two.

Clearly, the mind is a wondrous thing! However, if left to its own devices, your mind can also deceive you, mess you up, and trip you up badly!

Do you know what else it is really good at?

It's good at playing movies that loop over and over again and tell you why you are bound to fail, why you'll never make a go of your blue-sky idea, and how you should never leave an unhappy relationship because you'll be really lonely.

Yes, the mind is really good at making excuses, and making them sound so convincing that you believe that they are real!

Excuses that stop you from walking away from the ordinary and conventional path because you are afraid of what is around the corner.

Excuses that say you should keep doing the same thing over and over again because it's been done by your family and friends, so who are you to break the norm?

Excuses that keep you stalled where you are, because you don't have the time or the luck to break out, obscuring the reality that you make your own time and create your own luck.

Excuses that say you are a failure, and that a failure is all that you will ever be for the rest of your life!

When your mind acts that way, it's a virus!

It's a virus that spreads into all areas of your life!

If you feel that you are a failure in business, and you tell yourself that often enough, the sense of failure will spread to all other areas of your life. When that happens, you'll view every single setback as a disappointment and loss, offering further proof of what you already know— that you are a failure!

Someone else with a more positive mindset will view an obstacle or impediment as a challenge or a gift, but when your mind repeatedly drills into you that you are a disappointment, it will become a self-fulfilling prophecy. You may become a defeatist and throw your hands up at even the smallest difficulty.

You may procrastinate at work and miss deadlines, thereby botching your chances of a promotion.

You may handle your work carelessly because what you do isn't very good anyway, so why bother and why care?

Not surprisingly, when you let this mindset get its way, you will ignore any achievements that you may have, and you only look at life through the lens of failure.

That is what happens when a virus attacks, it hijacks a healthy cell and uses its mechanism to create even more viruses to assault and corrupt other cells.

Your despairing attitude may have originated from growing up with harsh parents, who found fault with every single thing that you did. It could have been rooted in a key trauma in your life, such as being in school and not fitting in, or being bullied by kids of your own age, or that you were so broken up by a bad relationship that you think that you are not worth anything . . . or worth very little!

Additionally, when your mind is invaded by fear and negativity, you'll worry about why people don't like you, and you'll go into a tailspin of anxiety that undercuts your confidence. When that happens, you'll slide even further into doubt and you will never achieve your dreams because by that time, you are unable to carve your own path.

You'll be so convinced that dreams and aspirations are for other people, not for you, that you'll stay exactly where you are. Bright hope is replaced by grey pessimism, and "can do" is swapped out for "why bother." You stay stuck in misery but refuse to admit that you are in pain!

My mind did something similar to me when it came to my marriage.

I recall desperately wanting to leave a marriage that no longer worked and no longer supported me. I knew with every fibre of my being that it was over and that my husband deserved to be with someone else who could truly love him.

I was compelled to find my own path but it took me five years to leave, during which time I was chronically unhappy.

I came up with every possible excuse:

What about the kids?

How do we split our assets? (We sold a very successful retail company, in a bidding war between two publicly listed companies, and we did very well with the sale.)

What if I am afraid of being alone?
How do I start dating again?
What if I never find someone again?
Am I doomed to always be single from now on?
The excuses went on and on!
Has that happened to you?

Have you used up so much time and energy creating excuse after excuse, that you have no internal resources left to grab the opportunity that life throws your way?

Meanwhile, like what happened to me, your body is screaming for your attention and sending signals that this is just not working out. I continued to suffer debilitating pains in my stomach and I endured anxiety and depression.

Would you believe that my mind rationalized the messages from the body as something related only to my body and not to my overall being, which wasn't at all happy, nor to my self-esteem . . . which was running pretty thin by that time!

I was disconnecting my mind from my heart and from my spirit, and I paid the price for it!

Meanwhile, the excuses kept piling on until the day when I just couldn't take it anymore. I could have left my husband sooner and made the best of my time. Instead, I languished in an increasingly painful, argumentative, and abusive marriage.

We had married young. I had dropped out of school because the psychology professor said I wasn't in the right place and didn't belong in the ranks of his students. I had the answers to the questions and quizzes posted in the tests, but they weren't answers that fit in nicely with the conventional mindset.

Even though we did not struggle financially, and the opportunities always showed up, the money created its own set of problems!

I had subconsciously subscribed to my family's paradigm that money was bad!

My parents belonged to the middle class and rather than viewing money as a positive resource that can be leveraged to do more, and to give us more choices, they had an unhappy and unhealthy relationship with money.

My dad had no real teachings for me around money, and my mother was constantly stressed out about where money was going to come from. This was based on her own experiences with my grandmother, as well as her living on welfare for a brief time when we were children.

Therefore, I had established a relationship of scarcity with money. It was to be feared and I was to be in lack! I knew how to make it . . . but keeping it was a totally different matter!

When I prospered financially, rather than receiving congratulations from the people surrounding me, all I received was envy and jealously. They kept saying to me, "Must be nice to be so young and have all this money," or "Must be nice to live in this big house and have these nice cars." It was a lot of "Must be nice . . . " statements, which often ended with an accusation that surely, since I had so much, I should be giving more away!

I felt horrible! I had somehow figured out a way to create wealth but without consciously thinking about it, I had bought into my family's energetic struggles around money. Here I was, wealthy and young, dealing with jealousy and envy from the people closest to me, as well as dealing with a broken marriage.

I kept only enough cash for a down payment on my house when I left the marriage.

I felt such deep, intense, shame and guilt at earning all that money when I was so young. I was running a lot of subconscious programs in my mind that I had done something wrong by being successful.

Rather than finding ways to create more wealth and abundance with what I was given, I found a creative way to get rid of it—through a bad marriage and bad financial investments.

I remember that the day my husband moved out of our family home, it was as if a massive weight had lifted off my shoulders. I felt the negative energy leave me. I'll never forget that sense of incredible lightness of being. Someone had lifted a massive burden of bricks off of my shoulders.

It felt like the coolest thing ever, even though nothing physical had been taken off of me. That feeling was accentuated when I slept in my new home.

I remember the night that the movers came. They messed up the instructions and only sent two men and a small truck. We were unloading until 3 o'clock in the morning, by which time I was fully and wholly exhausted!!

That first night, I grabbed a cover and slept curled up on the floor. However, it didn't matter that it was a hard floor—I slept so well and my body felt light, buoyant, and weightless.

Crazy, isn't it? Getting my best sleep in years on a hard floor, snuggled and wrapped up in a blanket!

The marked sensation of moving from being burdened to weightlessness also started me questioning my preconceptions, and everything that I had been schooled to believe.

Thus began my exploration into energy and energy- based healing work.

It started because I asked the question, "How can I feel a weight discernibly lifted off of me if energy is not real?"

Taking Back Control of Your Mind

Did you know it has been proven that most people gravitate to what they know, and shy away from what they do not know?

You see it repeatedly and you may have seen it in your own life. You may like to walk the familiar path, making the same decisions and repeating the same mistakes. You only care to do what you have been schooled in and taught by those around you.

You are afraid to take a risk because if you fail, you are considered a loser amongst family members and peers . . . or even to yourself!

You force yourself to fit in, even though it pains you. It's like forcing yourself to wear old shoes that no longer fit because it's something you have known all of your life.

Why does the mind come up with excuses to stop you from moving forward?

Very simply, it likes hanging out in its comfort zone. It hates being evicted out of what is familiar. It resists stress and pressure, and it will usurp any attempts to change. That is when the mind comes up with the most damaging excuses so that things will stay the same!

Who Has the Password to Your Mental Wi-Fi?

Let's say that someone scammed you and retrieved the login information and password to your bank account. That would be a downright disaster, wouldn't it? You would most definitely be distraught and you would do whatever you could to fix it.

Yet you willingly surrender the keys to your mind, and to your energy field, and let people take away your energy. You don't even think twice about it!

What if you lost your cell phone or it stopped working? I bet you would run down to the corner store and get it fixed as soon as possible. You might even have mild anxiety until you have it functioning again. So why don't you treat your body, your spirit, your mind, and your soul like that . . . with as much care as you would a device?

For example, have you ever walked into a room where the tension is so thick that you can cut it with a knife? When the atmosphere is so filled with anger and resentment that you feel it all over your body like an uneasy, clammy feeling or a tingling up and down your spine?

Nothing physical is present to suggest that there is something wrong, but you pick up on the negative frequencies anyway.

Every emotion that a person gives off is a frequency. In most cases, people brush off those negative vibes but if you are more sensitive and more vulnerable, and you don't have strong enough boundaries, you will get upset and disturbed right away. You will allow their energy to immediately penetrate your field and you'll feel different in the room, compared to how you felt just before you walked in. This collective energy in the room becomes the virus that enters your mental, emotional, and spiritual fields. You are now infected!!

When you walk your own path you will inevitably come across critics who judge you, and haters who are so envious of you, that they shame you. What do you do when that happens?

Some people become people-pleasers. They want everyone to like them, and in the process, they give too much weight to the opinions of others, and reject their own values.

Such people may be wired at a very deep level to please others in order to avoid bearing the brunt of their anger or being physically hurt. They may people-please because they are afraid of being rejected because that means, to them, that they have been weighed, judged, and found wanting.

Understand that it is NOT your job to make people feel good! Your responsibility is to yourself! People-pleasing erodes your boundaries and may have an unfortunate backlash. You may end up resenting the very same people that you are trying to please because they are taking you away from what you want to do. Think about what being a people-pleaser costs you, it takes away your self-confidence and increases internal stress.

Build stronger boundaries and strike a balance between short-term disequilibrium, from not pleasing someone, and long-term personal freedom. Be picky about who you hang out with . . . BE PICKY!

Honour your inner knowing and how you feel! Be brave to say "No, thank you!," and be amazing at loving yourself!

Don't bring yourself down to the level of those who judge you. Don't drop your standards to accommodate those who refuse to up-level theirs to match yours!

Don't waste time explaining what it is that you seek for yourself. Those who love you will accept the path that you carve for yourself and those who don't, aren't worth bothering about anyway!

Train your mind to do BETTER! Train it to choose to see the upbeat and the positive. Train it to reject the doom and gloom. Remember, every second is a point of choice! The choices you make in those moments lead to certain outcomes in your life.

Ask yourself this question every day: "What am I truly ready to choose differently? Today, what can I choose that is different, so that I can have something different, wonderful, and positive show up in my life?"

Your mind can be trained . . . or retrained! You can shape it to see the good in every experience. The first step in overcoming a mind-set of failure or disappointment, is to fully realize that it exists and that it has been controlling and colouring your response to every experience. The second step is to recognize that you don't have to believe what it says. Change the filter!

See every new experience, and every new opportunity that comes your way, as a way to wipe the slate clean and start afresh. Your previous mistakes can be your teacher. They can teach you to act differently, but they are not you, and you are not the sum total of your mistakes. You are much more than that!

Remember that when you live from the heart, it takes over the mental thoughts that assail you. So many people run around saying, "What do I think?" without recognizing that the mind is where you have placed your power, and that it's usually running from subconscious programming. Instead, when asked, "What do I feel?" your heart takes over.

Bang! . . . the heart takes charge of the mental thoughts and you immediately create better experiences and outcomes, with the added bonus that your mind becomes more peaceful and free! Your brain has two sides and if you let your mind control your operating system, you will always get a right and wrong answer to any question that you ask . . . if you dwell too long in overthinking!

Learn to feel, and learn to take charge of the mind, so that it does not become a virus!

I didn't finish school with a lot of accolades, but I learned from running a successful business that being different was the correct way for me. Embrace the fact that you are different!

Love yourself for being off-kilter, and go boldly forward in the direction of your dreams!

Don't let the haters and the critics tell you otherwise and DON'T surrender your empowerment to them! Take action as only you know how!

It is when you ACT that you gain new knowledge and new insights! You will walk into a new way of being, a new way of breathing, and a new way of thinking!

For those people who give up on something without trying because they claim that it is not possible, ask yourself who it is that they are listening to—the voices of their parents, of their inner and outer critics, of people who are afraid? Chances are, if they explore further, they are just giving in to irrational and groundless fear!

When you are willing to take action in the face of the naysayers, and when you disregard those who mean well but project their fears onto you, the first few steps you take may be wobbly. You may feel terribly alone because you are leaving what is known and familiar behind.

However, when you keep on going with focus and courage, the impossible becomes possible! It no longer becomes an impossible dream. It is a vision that becomes real and the world will be a far better place because you dared to dream and to achieve!

Make a friend of your mind, but make sure it's aligned with your intuition and your spirit. Do not allow it to take the lead! When all parts of you work in harmony—mind, body, and spirit—and when the feeling centre has as much say as the mind, you open up to the healing energies of the Universe.

Trust yourself, and listen to your mind, body, and soul! If your mind chatters too much, drop down into your intuition and see what your feeling centre has to say.

Here are a few more tips to help you on your way:

- Trust yourself! Listen to your spirit, body, and soul!

- Understand that it is your life, and that you make it work, or fail, through the decisions and choices that you make every second of every day.

- Every day, make choices that reflect that you love yourself.

- Avoid overwhelm by listing out your priorities. Creating this list is tantamount to giving your mind a road map to move you forward.

- Understand that there is a solution to every problem that confronts you . . . stay focused!

- Be willing to turn over every stone, because there is a way around every obstacle that you come across in life.

- Question why something is not working and be open to the answer when it comes.

- Don't reject what is unfamiliar . . . just because it's new to you, doesn't mean that it doesn't work!

- Don't waste your time overthinking about this or that. If you are waiting for the perfect moment to start on something new, you'll likely never start at all!

- Tell yourself it's never too late to change for the better

- Be careful who and what you listen to

- Listen to music and stories that uplift and inspire you

- Turn off the news!

- Be willing to make mistakes! A mistake is not a failure, and really, failure is not the end of the world! It's just a way of telling you what to do differently next time.

- Learn how to connect to the God of your understanding, and have conversations with the God of your understanding every day!

- Learn how to follow the signs

- Learn how to TRUST in all that you cannot see with your eyes

Testimonial 5:
Seeing Myself As The Unseen Victim – From Victim To Victory!

Through the weekend workshop, I had a couple of hours where I "really" wanted to be on the Transformation seat. I wanted to be heard for whatever problem I had at the time (I honestly don't even remember what).

For about 2 hours I kept feeling like "I wasn't being picked" and that was poking at my "Being Unseen" void.

It was so cool, because, I would be listening, and then I would go into these (above) thoughts and feelings and I suddenly noticed I wasn't listening to anything that was being said.

My entire focus was on my/ mine/I.

I am so thankful for all the clearings of the weekend that are still coursing through me, because when I started to LISTEN, I realized that every person in the Transformation Seat was asking about things I wanted to ask about. There was not one person, who was moving through something that was irrelevant to me.

When this "seeing myself as the unseen victim" cleared for me, it was like I just woke up from a heavy hazy dream. All of this happened during the Sunday morning piece.

I realized this new level of making myself a victim and how it was safe. Blaming others for not seeing me, not "allowing" me to speak and such.

And not realizing that the Universe knows what I'm struggling with and my questions are LITERALLY being answered and cleared in that moment, but I'm tuned into my victim frequency, so I can't hear it. I am so thankful for the Hand of God changing my frequency and now I can HEAR it!

I was rejecting the clearing because I didn't get to ask. It wasn't coming in the way I wanted. I was also disconnecting from community and God in those few hours, because I had wanted to speak and share.

I am SO SO THANKFUL, to get kicked out of this deeply entrenched place and thought process.

And to everyone of you who was in the Transformation Seats - thank you thank you thank you! You guys pulled up and out TONS of old programming. You are brilliant and perfect and stunningly beautiful in your journey!

This whole weekend was absolutely perfect for me and was more than what I required.

Thank you again Tracy L Clark!

So much love everyone!!

Aarti Mathur

Chapter 6

Stop Cursing Your Life;
You're on the Brink of a Miracle!

"Every day, you send noise into the atmosphere via your thoughts and words. Are you sending negativity or love? Choose wisely!"

– Tracy L Clark

It wasn't until I was much older that I realized that I was cursing my life, by thinking and speaking negative words, and I was doing it on a daily basis.

I finally had the epiphany that the life that I was living right at this moment, had been created a long time ago by the words that I had chosen way back then to describe who I was, how I was, and why I was. I wish that I had learned or known as a child that this power rested within me, that when we speak good into our lives, we bring in new blessings!

However, from a young age I was never told that I was a co-creator. By emulating daily the dysfunctions that were happening around me, I focused instead on what was missing in my life, what was currently in my life that I didn't want, and why I was burdened with so many illnesses and problems.

Cursing My Life

You know by now that the school system just didn't work for me. It was very difficult for me to sit through the boring curriculum. Deep down, I knew that something did not sit right with me. I could feel unease but it was only when I grew older that I recognized that it wasn't just the boredom of school that I was rejecting.

I was forcefully, albeit subconsciously, rejecting the programming that the schooling institution was drumming into my own system and my own consciousness.

On some level, I clearly understood that the teaching would not help me much in life. If you are not one to follow the crowd, no matter how young or old you are, you will feel that you are a stranger in a strange land.

I yearned to know more but my interests ran to more esoteric topics, like how the Star Trek crew beamed themselves in and out of sticky situations, and fantasy worlds where there were aliens, fairies, and angels, zipping around doing wondrous things!

Perhaps if instead of dealing with boring triangles and trigonometry, the schools had taught sacred geometry and the architecture of ancient sites, I would have aced my school work. Instead, I struggled very hard just to get Bs and Cs. I was told to slog through the mundane and boring classes but inside of me, I resisted.

Where was school going to get me? It would get me to where my family was and to what my family was doing—which was nothing inspirational because their lives were more of a slog.

So I escaped, I took to dancing!

I was the poor kid in a dance studio catering to rich girls and the only reason that I could get in, was because my stepfather worked with the dance teacher's husband.

The rich girls were so mean and they would say cruel and horrible things to me every time I was in the studio.

As such, even though I was enjoying the dancing, I was afraid when I was in the studio and I was afraid to fight back, as some more confident kids might have done.

There was so much anger in my family, and I was afraid to step into my truth and speak up because I didn't want to be yelled at anymore.

When I was 13 years old, I would go on tirades about my body. I tirelessly called myself fat, even though in truth I was not, and I was petrified of being overweight.

I would always be angry with myself. I kept describing myself as ugly, and telling myself that I wasn't good enough or smart enough (since I didn't get any A's in school), and that there was no way anyone would want to be with me because I had nothing special to offer.

Maybe they would reject me too because according to my dance mates, I was born on the "wrong side of the tracks!"

I chose to listen to depressing music, as all I wanted to do was to zone out because my life was so miserable. I kept saying to myself, "Look at you; you are hideous, you are stupid, you are dumb!" These were very harsh words—I know that to be true now—but as a teenager, I had no model of positivity, love, or kindness to look up to.

All around me were people who were sick, couples who were breaking up from unhappy marriages, families who were being kicked out of their homes, and peers who didn't hesitate to cruelly label me as being stupid and abnormal.

No one around me ever taught me, or helped me to change my perspective, to look at what was right about me. As such, I bought into it, hook, line, and sinker, that I was not of any worth. That was my world for the first part of my life. I withdrew and shrank into my shell like a turtle would.

When I hit my late teens, I swung to the other extreme. I partied hard in high school to escape the pain of my reality. The loud music and alcohol numbed the pain that I felt about not being loved and not feeling safe.

The people around me didn't understand why I would be lacking in self-confidence and self-esteem because in their eyes, I was so pretty, and surely I was the belle of the ball!

I walked around constantly saying that everyone was against me.

No matter how hard I worked or struggled, I would be railing at the heavens as to why I kept attracting negative people into my life, people who brought me abuse and heartbreak.

I didn't know about the power behind words and what our words can do to us. I wasn't aware that our words can ail us, or regenerate us, and how quickly and powerfully they become our reality!

As much as I was playing the victim, I was doing it to myself. I was creating this world of pain and suffering, modeling my reality on what was presented to me in my daily environment, and I kept on doing more of the same.

I was cursing my life in the present, and sowing seeds for a wretched life in the future! I felt like I was a victim of my illnesses, my upbringing, and my inability to do well at school. I didn't understand that I was personally responsible for the shape that my life was taking.

It's a notable trait of the victim that he or she sheds personal responsibility . . . and blames someone else!

One of the things that I learned from being so sick for such a large part of my life, and having a variety of illnesses, was that I made my sicknesses my friend. I talked incessantly about how much pain I was enduring, how I always needed to be close to a bathroom and how inconvenient that was, and how I was suffering. Whether it was the irritable bowel syndrome, diverticulitis, or ulcers, those ailments became my friend.

They were my tools to get attention and to get out of responsibilities.

Do you know someone like that?

Someone who makes a friend out of his or her illnesses to get attention and love?

I was the queen at this—a real diva! It is how I got a pass out of a humdrum existence and the pain of life.

Think about it, even in today's world the only way one truly gets a pass to pause and take a breath is to be sick. You can get a day, or even weeks, off of work or school. Try saying to your boss or your teacher that you don't want to come in today because you need a break. That is absolutely not acceptable, and you can only get the day off when you are ill.

I have seen many souls attract illness to themselves just so they could get out of their work and their life!

Everyone has a story. It's the "story" that we believe and play over and over again in our mind that moulds us into who we are. We are conditioned to wallow in our fears, anxieties, and traumas, talking about them like a rundown record! We sit in the pain and we become so attached to the anguish and the agony that it becomes a part of us, and like all victims do, we leverage the trauma to get a pass in life.

We get people to think of us as "Poor you! You have it so rough . . . can I help?"

We appeal to people's inclination to root for the underdog and those down on their luck. We suffer under the delusion that when we show that we are suffering, we are able to get attention from our friends and family, not really understanding that at some point they will tire of it, and then we will look for a different audience to listen to our woes.

After all, in school or at work, when you are sick you get a day off. If you hate the life that you are leading, but don't believe that you have the ability to change it, your body will break down in some manner or another. You may suffer depression, anxiety, chronic fatigue, insomnia, addiction, or a condition that just saps your energy and warps your life.

Your body gets the signals that you send to it: "I hate this life! I don't want any more of it! I want out!"

There is a wonderful quote from Deepak Chopra: "Every cell in your body is eavesdropping on your thoughts." I might add that they are listening in on your words too!

At last count, scientists believe there are 73 trillion cells in your body. That number keeps increasing as science becomes more technologically sophisticated in mapping out the miracle that is the human body. Let me put it this way, 73 trillion of anything packs a mighty punch, and your body does exactly what you tell it to do!

You may think that you get sick due to only external factors, such as pollution and nutrient-deprived, genetically modified food. Yes, the external environment does matter, but the internal environment carries a whole lot more weight!

Everyone is so consumed by looking outside of themselves for answers but the plain truth is that you have to go inside to find the guidance that you long for. In you resides the keys to unlocking the good, the abundance, the love, and everything for which you are asking.

When you clean up on the inside, you create space for the new to come in!

Seeing Through the Pain

Let's flip this around!

So often, you look outside of yourself to pin the blame for your ills on someone but the reality is that it is all about you!

YOU are the one putting the words out there and YOU are the one sculpting your life with what you think and how you feel, not those around you! Those around you are only reflecting back what you are putting out there.

Once you understand that, you can move on!

Don't use the pain as a crutch to get more attention!

Instead, use the pain as a motivating factor to get off your butt! Rather than stewing in sickness or trauma, affirm these statements to yourself:

I am stronger than this!
I am better than this!
I am healthy!
I am pain free!
I reclaim my birthright now!

You have to stand up to your traumas because they are familiar to you, and they like hanging around because of the attention they garner. Stand up to them, deliver them eviction notices, and get them out of your life!

Ban them from your energy field!

This is what my clients accomplish with the Body Regeneration Method™ that I teach.

Without evicting your pain points, your life becomes a game of snakes and ladders. You are making good progress, and then you hit a snake and you fall right back to zero.

You may be hoping to heal, and you see some forward movement, but your thoughts about your illnesses remain the same. Soon enough, they surface, your body reacts to the negative message, and you are back where you first started.

I have gone to many therapists and I noticed that they insisted on revisiting a pain point or trauma in my life over and over again, each time anchoring it even more deeply in my body. Every time you say, "I have _____" (any condition or disorder), your cells hear what you are saying, and they reaffirm that you have this or that disease by giving you more of it!

Instead, use a more positive, forward-looking affirmation, such as "I am doing the right thing. Thank you, God! I command the illness out of my body now!"

Purging yourself of the old hateful vocabulary, and changing to positive thoughts and statements, is the first step. Next, you have to go within to talk to your body.

Here is a simple exercise.

Throughout the next day or so, ask your body to show you where it is hiding pain or stress. Invite it to open up to you, and stay mindful to the subtle physical messages!

During the day, you may feel a denseness somewhere or an ache that you've never noticed before, it's your body answering you!

Every part of your body is functionally linked to your emotions. Your respiratory organs, your lungs, deal with breathing in the life force energy. If they are not working as they should be and you are experiencing allergies, asthma, or other respiratory problems, in essence what the illness is saying is that you are being smothered by life. It's too much for you, and you can't breathe.

Look around your life, what are you finding hard to process? Under what circumstances are you afraid to breathe? What forces you to hold your breath in, and what makes you hyperventilate?

As you walk through your life every day, pay attention to such cues from your body, and you will find the answers inside of you!

I had a client who had an annoying cough. He was incessantly coughing. He had never been able to express his point of view throughout his marriage and at that point, his marriage had come to an end. However, after 30 years of not speaking up, he was hampered by the programming that dwelled deep inside of him.

I said to him, "You are having issues speaking your truth to your wife, and you do not feel heard. This needs to change because the marriage is not working anymore!"

What he perceived to be love in his marriage was not love. They were both just going through the motions. Previous attempts to mend the relationship had failed and it was time for them to go their separate ways.

Guess what?

When the marriage broke up, the cough went away as well.

Yes, his wife was the cause of the cough because the dynamics of the relationship were not keeping pace with his own changes.

Listen to your body's wisdom! Notice how and where your body reacts to people, issues, and challenges. When you change your relationship with such people, and face up to your challenges, your body will repair!

I had stomach problems throughout my life. I had been trapped in stressful environments and I was always on edge! I couldn't relax and my body acted as if it was always on guard. When I left my marriage and moved into a small home that became my safe sanctuary, my stomach issues went away within three months.

Growing up, my life was high-stress and then I moved into a high-stress marriage. When I finally said, "NO MORE!" and left the dysfunctional environments behind, my body was able to relax, to let go, and find the space to repair itself.

Now once in a while, very rarely, I will have a stomach issue. When that happens, I take the time to observe who or what has come into my space that is prompting this reaction from my body. Once I hit on the answers, I make the appropriate changes and the problem goes away immediately!

Your body KNOWS, it is always listening, don't doubt its wisdom!

Your stomach and associated organs, the gut area, deal with processing life and its ups and downs. When you can process what life hands to you, you are able to act proactively. However, if you can't take life in its abundance, you'll probably suffer tummy or gut disorders.

Your reproductive organs are your power zone and the source of your creativity. If they are in trauma, think about how much of your own power you are surrendering to someone else, to an institution, or to a set of beliefs that don't support you!

Is there a part of you that thinks you are unworthy and incapable?

Are you jealous of others who are more successful than you?

Are you not trusting your own talents?

How have you disempowered yourself?

Think on this, at this particular moment you may not be at the weight that you desire, nor be holding the job that grabs your passion.

Rather than indulging in saying that you are too fat or too unaccomplished, shift the direction of your life path by switching to words that are thankful and welcoming—like with this prayer:

"Thank you, God, for that wonderful job of my dreams!

Thank you for bringing into my life the person who loves and honours me!

Thank you for restoring my health and vitality!

Thank you, God, for this beautiful and powerful body that I get to walk in each and every day.

And even better, even better, and even better!"

When you speak words of positivity into your life, even though what you are describing is not in your life right now, you are short-circuiting your old, negative, words and ways that have created your life up until this point. You are sowing the seeds to blossom into the new life that you want!

It takes practice to create a new habit!

In the beginning, you may have negative thoughts running rampant through your mind, just like they have been doing for all of your life. That's okay, be kind and be patient!

Remember, creating a new program can be difficult, or it can be easy, it's all about your choice!

If you can override your tendency to go back towards the familiar, and FEEL the new words that you are speaking, your life will change as you desire it!

There is a quote that says "where attention goes, energy flows." Turn your attention to the good things that you want, not the bad things that you currently have!

I like to say that your world is like a garden, you get out of it, what you put into it!

If you picture beautiful thoughts like strong, rooted trees, you'll receive beauty and strength. If your garden gets all choked up with pessimism, jealousy, or lack of self-confidence, it will choke out the rest of the life in your garden like weeds!

You need to weed out the negative thoughts, feelings, and words. You can't carve out a different life experience if you keep doing and saying the same things that you were thinking and doing before, because when the reality doesn't change in the way that you expect, you'll get sad, frustrated, and feel empty.

Stop talking about the past!

That is like carrying luggage that you no longer require into your present and into your future. I encourage you to listen carefully to what you speak and how you say it.

This simple tool can shift your entire reality at light speed!

Don't Give Up Before the Miracle Arrives!

Many days I wanted to give up believing that I was going to have a restored body, but deep inside of me I kept hearing, "Do not give up! Keep going! Keep focusing on the miracles that have happened. Keep trusting and keep believing!"

When my head shook so badly from the damaged nerves that it looked as if I was going into a seizure, I never gave up on finding the solution. I could have taken the easy way out by telling myself that I had a tic and that I had to live with it for the rest of my life, even though the pain in my neck would be so excruciating that all I wanted to do was rip my head off to stop the agony . . . but I didn't!!

As a child, the attacks happened out of the blue and I was the subject of much scorn with my bobble-head, rapidly twitching eyelids, and shaking limbs, but I refused to give in!

I felt that I deserved a better life, one without the tics, spasms, and pain!

Through energy work and a conscious program to control my stress, I stopped the quivering in my arms and the fluttering of my eyelids. I could have given up at this point.

My head was still shaking and the pain was beyond anything that I can explain but getting two out of three sorted out wasn't a bad batting average. I said to myself, "No way am I settling for less! This is MY body and I am not going to live like this!"

I searched and scoured all over for healing modalities and I tried everything that felt right. My body was telling me that my disorder was linked to feeling unsafe in my environment and to how I reacted to stress. Yes, there was a physical and mechanical issue, but the head tics were still linked to my stress levels.

I was determined to be fully healed and I never lost sight of my goal!

Eventually, I was led to an osteopath, ten years after my journey began! I had energetically gotten rid of the nervous tics in my arms and my eyes.

However, I knew that I needed to keep searching and when I found him, he immediately diagnosed my ailment as pectus evectum. No one else had been able to figure this out and on hearing those words, I realized that I had found the right soul. I was so relieved when he perkily said, "Yes, I can help you!"

A week later I went back to him for the adjustments, which caused me a lot of pain, but my head has never shaken again since!

There was a scene in the movie The Pursuit of Happiness, starring Will Smith, where the son tells the father a joke. It goes something like this:

There is a man drowning in the ocean, and he cries out to the heavens, "God, please help me!"

A boat comes along and the crew says, "Sir, let us help you!" and the man answers, "No, God will save me!"

The boat sails off and a second boat comes along. The sailor says, "Sir, let me help you!" and the drowning man says yet again, "No, God will help me!"

The man dies and goes to Heaven.

In Heaven he asks, "God, why didn't you save me?" and God replies:

"I sent you two boats!"

How often have you asked for a miracle, and yet you passed over the answer that was presented to you because you thought that you knew better, and consequently you stayed in pain and distress for longer than you needed to?

God hears you and sends you the answers that you need, in the same way that He led me to the osteopath.

I LISTENED, I HEARD, I FELT, and I KNEW! . . . that he was the right guy to fix me!

God WILL answer you! . . . . however you must be willing to listen and act accordingly!

I have come a very long way to get my body back on track, my mind aligned with its true potential, and my spirit to be of service. Along the way, I have learned a few lessons to guide you on your own healing journey, which I would like to share with you here:

- Embrace the illness! Love, love, love your illness! Stop rejecting it, and stop cursing it!

- Thank it for the lessons it is showing you and make the required changes!

- Embrace the beauty all around you!

- Embrace the beauty inside of you!

- Stop looking outside, and look inside. The answers will guide your next steps.

- Stop comparing yourself to others, they too have challenges in their lives.

- Let go of the frequencies of illness. Give it back to God! When you release the frequencies, new possibilities arise within to restore your body.

- Take charge of your life! Don't settle for one diagnosis or answer, especially when it doesn't sit right with you.

- Be the Sherlock Holmes of your life. Be willing to keep looking for what works.

- Never stop believing!!!

- Keep asking the questions, keep following the answers, and follow your inner knowing!

- Let go of expectations!

- Trust that the miracle is on its way to you right now, and that it is already done!

- TRUST in what you cannot see!

- BELIEVE in what you cannot see!

- KNOW without a shadow of a doubt, that God has this, and that it is already done!

So often when we are starting something new, we get frustrated when the results are slow in coming, or we are disappointed when we see only small changes. Be patient . . . the miracle is on its way to you!

The seeds have been planted and the body needs to process the adjustments, and catch up to your new way of speaking and being.

So many of you give up right before the miracle or the breakthrough arrives because you mistakenly believe that the small, incremental changes that you see are the final result. Does this sound familiar?

Influenced by our quick-fix, short-attention-span society, we are impatient for results. That impatience comes with a big cost! Impatience gives way to disbelief and we shoot ourselves in the foot by prematurely ending the recovery process. When I was looking to heal my nervous system, there were so many times that I just wanted to stop, throw in the towel, and just live with the tremors and the incredible pain.

However, I kept hearing the inner, soft voice telling me that since I had managed to repair my arms and eyes, I would be able to find the solution for my head. So, I made peace with my body instead of fighting it!

I gave thanks every day for the miracle that was coming my way . . . and then it arrived!

In your healing journey, you have to let go of expectations on what shape the miracle will take, who will help you and when, and when the miracle will arrive. Expectation doesn't do anything except create a dissatisfaction or a dissonance within us, which inadvertently interferes with the healing that God gives to us.

It's not just your expectation that may blindside you. Stay immune to well-meaning comments from people who say such things as, "Well, you've been waiting forever and you are right where you started." They may mean well, but such people are projecting their own ideas and concepts of what healing should look like.

Such comments create doubt within your energy field and within your body. Your conviction lags, your determination wilts, and your body echoes those sentiments by re-enacting feelings from past failures. When faced with such overwhelming obstacles, you give up.

Yet for all you know the miracle that you long for, and have worked towards, is right around the corner!

Remember, it is your own life-changing experience which you navigate on your own terms and at your own speed. You don't need to carry anyone else with you, or be saddled with their opinions, no matter how much they love you. When people share their projected opinions, I love to say, "Thanks for sharing!" and then walk away or say nothing more.

The energy will drop and you will not absorb it.

You've done everything you need to, you've changed your vocabulary, you've immersed your mind, body, and spirit in positive thoughts, but you feel that you can do with some help because the road of self-transformation can seem long and winding.

What do you do then?

This is where gratitude and faith come in, both of which are discussed in the final chapters of the book. You are only human and regardless of how committed you are to your healing journey, you are bound to come across a glitch in the matrix here and there. Don't berate yourself when that happens and don't judge yourself so harshly.

Instead, tap into gratitude and faith!

Those are the God-given qualities that you need to lend you speed and energy to get to the new wondrous life, and well-being that you desire.

They will help you to embrace the process, boost your emotional strength, and transmute your challenges to strengths.

Testimonial 6:
Tracy Changed Our Lives And The Miracles Flowed!

Tracy, where do Rob and I even start and how can we even begin to thank you? You have changed and impacted every single facet of our lives! For almost 20 years, I was in excruciating pain and could not move my neck. The doctors and specialists told me that they would have to operate and fuse my vertebrae to ease the pain but that I would never have full range of motion again.

One session with you and you released the trauma that was stuck, and my neck is fully healed! The doctors have no idea how I am better!

My husband and I never thought that we would be able to come to terms and be at peace with the death of our daughter. Thank you, Tracy, for helping us move through and be grateful for one of the most difficult challenges of our lives.

I never thought that I would be able to let go of the rage, anger, and trauma that I held from a 6-year physically, mentally, and emotionally abusive relationship. Thank you, Tracy, for releasing me and freeing me from the pain and anger that had consumed me and created debilitating illness in my life.

My husband and I used to scrape together change to put gas in our car, our debt load was crushing, and we almost lost our house. Today, we are more prosperous than we ever thought possible, and money miracles show up almost daily! Thank you, Tracy, for opening our financial flow, and for changing our relationship with money.

Rob had served in the military for 20 years. He had been medically released from the military with severe back and knee injuries, PTSD, anxiety, depression, and severe panic attacks. All specialists said that he would be using a walker or a cane, and that his back and knee issues would only worsen; there was nothing that they could do for him. His panic attacks and PTSD from the military were debilitating and affected him every day. Through working with you, he is now fully healed of all physical, mental, and emotional issues. The doctors have no explanation for how Rob and I have healed!

Thank you from the bottom of our hearts for everything that you have done, and continue to do for us! Rob and I have no idea where we would be today if we had not met you in 2012. You are such a blessing to this world! You are such a blessing to us, and we would not have the life we have today without you. We are forever grateful!!!

So much love and blessings,

Julie and Rob Laird

Chapter 7

Let Go of Fear to Rebuild Your Foundation

"Don't fear what you don't know; you may be missing something amazing on the other side!"

– Tracy L Clark

The opposite of love is fear!

Fear is a four-letter word, and like most four-letter words, it should be purged from your vocabulary because it screws up your plans and sabotages your dreams . . . if you allow it to!

If you give into fear and let it get the better of you, it paralyzes you and keeps you in stasis, which stops you from realizing your visions, your dreams, and your life's work. If you harness it properly, fear can be a powerful motivating factor that pumps adrenalin into you and gives you the strength to scale new heights.

For most people though, fear stops you dead in your tracks. You may have an inner calling or a big dream that requires that you take a big leap of faith. However, you walk to the edge, take a look at how wide the chasm is, how deep the fall is, and you turn back, too afraid to make the jump into the unknown. You console yourself by saying it was too risky, that you have too much riding on yourself, and that you shoulder too many responsibilities to take on such a high risk.

Those are just excuses!

Excuses that you create to justify not finding enough courage or enough faith within you to step outside of your comfort zone. Instead, you let fear make the decision for you!

In some other cases, you wait for external validation that this is the right step to take—maybe a flash of lightning to light up your way, but that doesn't happen so you keep waiting.

One of the things that you must be aware of, is that fear is programmed into you from the time that you are conceived. It is like a game you need to navigate. Think about all of the arguments, the television, the schools, your family, and all of the conversations that you have had. How many times have you said "I am afraid of_____"

There is programming that says you are afraid to lose your money, lose your family, lose your friends, lose your freedom, lose your rights or your safety, and the list goes on!

Our society programs you to be in fear every day . . . rather than love!

Therefore, you can imagine why it is so difficult to purge from your system.

Here is the sad part about this reality. You either do or you don't, and when faced with such a situation, there are really only three feasible options:

- You say yes, you jump, and your dreams come to life!

- You say yes, you jump, you fall, you dust yourself off, get back up to your jumping off point, and your dreams are manifested!

- You turn back, you never know whether you have what it takes to succeed, and you look with great envy and jealousy at others who dare to make the jump.

In which camp do you belong?

The camp that says yes and goes for it . . . and maybe falters along the way but picks themselves up and keeps going for it no matter what??

Or are you in the camp that never gets what you want because you hug the sidelines?

How is it that we have created a world that is so full of fear?

Why is it that we are afraid of failing?

When did failure become a point of no return?

When did failure become so unforgivable a sin that you cannot recover from it?

Failure is nothing more than growing . . . plain and simple!

It should be encouraged because that is how you change quickly! However, you are taught in school that failure is bad and it prevents you from succeeding in life. Then the mind starts to adjust to this programming.

We all make mistakes, large and small, avoidable and unavoidable. Failure itself is not the problem. It only becomes an issue when you fail to learn from it, or you keep repeating the same mistakes over and over again. Most mistakes are unavoidable. Learn to forgive yourself by looking at your errors as teaching moments.

It's really not a problem to make mistakes, it's only a problem if you never learn from them!

There is a wonderfully succinct Chinese proverb that goes like this:

"Failure is not falling down . . . it is refusing to get up!"

From a different culture, and a much more recent time, are these memorable words by author JK Rowling, who spoke on the "Fringe Benefits of Failure and the Importance of Imagination," in her 2008 Harvard commencement address. She said:

"Failure was a stripping away of the inessential. I stopped pretending to myself that I was anything other than what I was, and began to direct all my energy into finishing the only work that mattered to me."

Highly successful people who blaze trails into the new and the unknown are never afraid of failure! They make a friend of failure and they keep going back to what they were pursuing. They embrace every lesson as a learning and they tweak and fine tune what doesn't work.

There are only a handful of extremely successful people, but success is not reserved only for the 1%. It's reserved for you, when you put your heart into it, when you are prepared to break out and take a quantum leap, and when you are prepared to let go of fears and let go of expectations!

There is something else you need to release!

You must release attachments to old, musty belief systems that weren't yours to begin with, but were attached to you like barnacles, because you modelled your beliefs on what was around you when you were growing up.

What I am writing here is meant to expand your thought processes so that when you get to the end of the book, you will open up to the Divine energy that will flow through you, uplift you to a new level, manifest your deepest dreams, your biggest visions, and give you the sure-footedness to walk into a new life beyond imagining!

If you think it is too late in your life, or that you have too many commitments to start afresh, I am here to tell you that it's never too late, and that you are never too old!

When I left my husband, I took custody of the kids and I only had enough money for a down payment on a house, so I went back into the corporate world.

I had a hard time deciding what I truly wanted to do, but I did find my footing again. When I did so, I felt like I had my life back on track. Money was flowing again, friends were fun, and the ground beneath my feet felt solid and stable.

However, even though my life seemed to be great I knew, from deep within, that something else was calling to me. I went out searching for groups of like-minded people who were seeking a spiritual path. There weren't a whole lot at that time, only the odd meditation group here and there.

Although they did not totally interest me, it was through those circles that I was led to my mentor Olga, who is sadly no longer with us.

Olga taught me a lot about energy work and where it intersected with science. Her teachings motivated me to learn even more. My curiosity aroused, I studied intensively and the deeper I delved into energy work, the more I developed the ability to hear messages outside of the normal hearing range. I could also see visions, such as apparitions and people who have passed on, just as I did when I was a little girl. Occasionally, when I am conducting hands-on-healing on people, I will see figures that are not of this 3D reality, be they of their spirit guides, angels, or their loved ones who have passed away.

During this time my health was improving. I was regaining my self-respect and I decided to help and heal other people, starting with friends and family. I would work on them just for fun. Most people consider play as a game of tennis or a card game, my version was helping to heal people. I spent eight years doing this for fun and for play.

I was thrilled to see that people would get all excited when they positively shifted their energies. The people I worked on would ask me what it was that I was doing. Was it something like Reiki? and I would reply, "I can't put a name on it because I just follow the energy of your body and my inner knowing. I can't explain it, that's all there is to it!"

I wasn't following any traditional school of healing or teaching. It was just my own inner knowing, guided by a power much bigger than myself.

At the time, I called it Divine, little did I know the extent of this connection. I kept hearing a gentle voice say, "Do not doubt, because when you do, you head off in the wrong direction."

This was my life then, around 17 years ago. However, the Divine had other plans!

Around 11 years ago, as I kept learning and enjoying myself, I landed in a role that was very much like a dream job. I travelled, I had fun, and I was enjoying life, while always working on my healing and helping others because that was what I loved the most! My office was full of crystals and I noticed that some people would come in and never want to leave because the energies in my office felt so soothing.

Yet there would be others who couldn't even walk past the doorframe. They sensed that the energy in the room was uncomfortable for them. In this environment, I could see what others did not.

I noticed procedures in my company that didn't add up, so I asked the chief financial officer (CFO) about it. He shut me up by laying into me, "You're stupid! You're a woman, do your job! You don't know what you are talking about!"

I thought to myself, I might be stupid but I work with lawyers, and something still didn't add up. There was more to it than meets the eye and my suspicions were well-founded.

The company soon went under and I hid for six months, berating myself for digging myself into yet another hole.

How was this possible? Why was I involved in another failure? What was I not getting, that the Universe had to send me yet another lesson?

I was so ashamed and embarrassed as to how I had worked myself into yet another severe setback. How could I not have foreseen that it would turn out so badly? I was working with very powerful, authoritative men, so how could I have chosen so wrongly? The bottom line was this, I was still not following my inner knowing.

I doubted myself and as such, was not fully into my power.

The old insecurities cropped up and for the next six months, self-doubt threatened to overwhelm me. I just wanted to curl up in a ball and hide from the world. I went over and over it in my mind—how could I have yet another setback after all of the work I had done on myself? Little did I realize that God was answering my prayers, he was just answering it in a way differently from what I had expected!

Meanwhile, business contacts that I had developed during the course of my corporate job offered me some really big contracts. At the same time, some of the people that I had healed during those days when I was doing it for fun, approached me and asked if I would continue to do healing work on them, as they thought I was really, really good!

Faced with two options, I had to dig deep into myself to figure out which one was the best way forward.

You know, those times when you are having a pity party of one and you get into a conversation with yourself, hoping that the answers will bubble up during the monologue.

I did precisely that, I said to myself, "Tracy, what do you want to do? Do you want to sell your soul to the devil and go back to that world full of snakes and idiots? . . . or do you really want to follow your passion?"

I decided to follow my inner urges and to take a big leap of faith. It had always been evident to the people around me that I absolutely loved healing and energy work. Even in the office, my colleagues would observe that I spent more time talking about energy than I did about documents or business.

I clearly remember the day that I decided to take on clients for energy work, and was to be paid for it, to see how it would pan out.

As I was walking down the stairs in my home, I said, "Okay, God, I am going to take what I know and trust!"

I had barely finished thinking through the last word, when an indescribable peace descended over me and blanketed me like a warm, comforting cape, infusing all the cells in my body. It was a peace so profound that it stayed with me to this day.

That was the moment when my life changed!

Every day for the next few months, I felt as if I had an angel looking over my shoulder, showering me with trust, faith, and peace, and I would keep looking back to see if the angel would leave.

There are no words to adequately describe that sacred feeling, it can only be experienced! Trying to pin words to it would be like trying to explain what it's like to give birth to a baby. Language is too clumsy to adequately capture the tremendous feelings of unconditional and fierce love that a person feels when seeing a baby for the first time. You have to experience it yourself to fully understand it!

After that defining decision was made, people started showing up for my energy sessions and over the next year, they kept showing up. This has been the case for over 10 years and I now have several types of live events, including Body Regen, Soul Sunday, retreats, an online learning academy, and podcasts, . . . and it keeps on changing!

Had you asked me ten years ago if this would be my life now, I would have said no!

Of course, there were a few bumps here and there, but I soon got into the flow of being able to heal and then teach. I have changed my business from strictly individual sessions into educating people and empowering them to heal in all areas of their lives, from their bodies to their bank accounts!

I realize how everything is truly connected.

Had I not lost that corporate role, who knows if I would have ever left. It was comfortable, and sometimes God needs to make us uncomfortable to propel us into our dreams and visions. However, you need to be ready to not wallow in fear. You need to take the right action, you need to jump out of the swamp and into the ocean!

Now my dreams keep growing!

From speaking engagements and radio shows, to corporate events helping companies remove stress out of the work place.

From opening a ministry to show people in the world how amazing they are, to teaching them to question what is not working for them and why.

My dreams keep building and changing because Spirit's plan is much bigger than I could ever imagine!

All of this from a woman who had no faith, no trust, and could not even say the word GOD! It is when you totally surrender to the call deep inside of you, and step out of fear, that you open the gateway to the unlimited possibilities that God has waiting for you!

There was a certain beauty in realizing that I had all of this knowledge and power that I was suppressing, and when I decided to take a leap of faith to follow my passion, God took care of the details!

God is always working through me and through you!

So often, if you are like me, you just forgot because there is no one there to show you the way. This is why I love to teach, to impart to people that they are powerful, but that they need to put their fears and their old programming behind them!

I wasn't immune to my fears. While I was still agonizing over the two paths before me, I would get all caught up in concerns, "I have my kids, I've got to look after them, and I have to pay the bills" but I totally surrendered to going where love and passion led me. I told myself that if this healing work didn't work out, and it was not meant to be, then God would guide me to something else . . . it DID work out, but God guided me to expand it to something even bigger and better than I could have ever imagined!

I would like to reassure you that even after making the decision to pursue my passion, enough stuff came up that would have derailed me had I lost faith, or decided to change my mind halfway through making the leap!

During this time of building my business from scratch, I suffered some arthritis in my hip, which I identified as being linked to anger with my mom. Old anger that surfaced made it hard for me to get out of bed. I went to the doctor and asked for an x-ray to confirm the arthritis.

After reviewing the x-rays, the doctor agreed that I was feeling the onset of arthritis. I then worked on releasing my anger towards my mom. When I went back for another round of x-rays a few months later, the medical staff said that there was an error in the first set of x-rays, because they didn't detect any evidence of arthritis in the latest round!

Once I released that anger, it was gone within a matter of months!

I love to share such stories. Many people find them far-fetched . . . but they are true!!!

In working with clients, I had many issues come up that taught me to get better at my own self-care and to build sturdy boundaries. Over time, I morphed into loving serving others. During this time, I became so complete inside, and working with more people deepened this sense of completion even more. I don't need to do anything else except what I have chosen to do. I truly get out of the way and let God do all the work.

Stop trying so hard and start surrendering!

I have had people come up and tell me that they will not work with me or come to an event because I am far too happy.

I tell them I am sorry but I am not going to be unhappy just to appease them. I know what misery is like, I lived a miserable life for many years and I don't need to hang out there anymore. I always have a good laugh when I get such reactions because it demonstrates how stuck some souls can get in their own drama, and how jaded and conditioned they are by old programming. Happiness is contagious and you should always take as much of it as you can get!

Not to mention, happiness allows God to bring more miracles because on a vibrational scale, it attracts your desires faster than fear or anger!

One day I had a strong encounter with the Christ. Now, I am not religious, but I do love the Holy Beings! I was afraid to share with anyone how much I had fallen in love with the Christ as his energy started to flow through me. It was no longer me, I was just the vessel!

I was terrified that I would offend people and that they would think that I was religious. As I shared with my community, they embraced this beautiful presence that helps so many. What so many do not understand, is that the Christ has a powerful healing energy that is available to everyone, and it is man that has made him an exclusive club!

Recently, I had to overcome this fear of judgement. I realized that I had so many programs around old teachings in my system. When I broke them, life became even more magical! Every time you let go of a fear, energy is cleared for more blessings!

Never forget that!

You will find new fears to overcome, and with FAITH and TRUST, you will find the blessings that you so deserve!

One of my first goals, which I wrote down ten years ago, was to have 30 clients a week. I hit that target very quickly but it also dawned on me that having this schedule didn't allow me to have much of a life.

God brought me what I had asked for, and now I needed to ask for something new!

I changed my goals and changed them again. I gave myself permission to change my milestones and goals at any time, as long as I felt good about it, and to move the goalposts once I hit that achievement or when the target no longer felt right.

I was 38 years old when I lost my corporate job and took a plunge into the unknown.

It wasn't too late to make a change, even if most people would have balked at taking the risk that I did. I knew that trusting my faith and following what I loved would completely change my life, and it has, in ways that I wouldn't have dreamt were possible!

Had I taken the so-called "safe" path and settled for the corporate contracts, none of what I have now would have become a reality . . . and you wouldn't be holding this book in your hand!

On the path that I walk now, I am guided totally by faith!

It is important to remember that you can walk a faith-filled life and tread through the unknown in trust, or you can live in a fear filled life, sit on the fence, work, pay taxes, and die.

In the end, it is entirely your choice!

I encourage you to take the journey, even if you fall down. You will second-guess your path, even when it looks amazing, but keep going anyway!

I still second-guess things some days, and when I do, Spirit sends in a soul to say thank you with such grace and meaning that it expands my heart!

It is in such moments that the heavens open up to shower me with blessings, the energy shifts, and more miracles unfold!

What to Do if You Don't Know Any Better

How do you take the right action if you don't know any better?

What if your role models and your belief systems from childhood keep you entrenched in fear?

What if the people around you, your friends, family, and community know only fear, are afraid of failure, and dismiss chasing your passions as silly, wishful thinking?

How do you then take the first steps to breaking out of that mold?

I have found that people who are unconscious will repeat a certain way of thinking or behaving, even if in the past this combination has led to poor outcomes, or at best mediocrity. They keep doing things the same way and thinking the same thoughts, in the hope that next time the results would be different.

This, to me, is a form of insanity . . . and we have many insane people in this world!

It is better for them to follow unconscious and reactive behaviour, just because it has been done before, than to step out of the box and try something new!

Let me assure you, it's not a dead end!

The body works like a magnificent computer and it will guide you if you listen to it. When you find yourself frustrated, angry, and feeling lack, realize that it's your body's way of telling you that it's time for a change. When that happens, don't give in to the negative emotions that are linked to uncertainty and change.

Instead, leverage these emotions as a motivating force to help you explore different points of view or perspectives that you may never have considered before, and see what makes your body feel lighter or happier. Use your body's intuition as a litmus test on what works better for you.

Many of you have come across a friend or an acquaintance who is well-entrenched in a career. When you ask them if they are doing something that they love, they ruefully say no, but at the end of the day they get a pension and benefits, or it's too much work to change careers in mid-life or when the economy is undergoing a downturn. This comes from programming that you received as a child which insists that you have to go to school, get a stable job, pay your taxes, and wait until retirement to live life . . . maybe!

WOW!!!

What is humanity thinking when it insists on such a narrow life?

To these people I say, "Wake Up!"

You have an entire life ahead of you in which you can create so many wondrous things that would benefit the world! Be it a piece of art, a new technology, a beautiful song, or an inspiring book, you give it all up to receive a paycheck and a pension, which you may or may not receive because the stresses of being unhappy at work may lead to a damaging illness.

There are countless ways to embrace a new way of living but if you are not willing to take the steps, small or bold, to get to what you want, you will never live the life that you desire. You will finally retire but you will be sad, and possibly in ill health.

This is the same with unhealthy relationships. If you are one of those people who hang on to toxic relationships, it's likely that you have justified your decision by pointing to the amount of time that you have already invested in the relationship.

Meanwhile, you are slowly sliding into depression, or anger, or anxiety, and your body is screaming at you to get out because it's starving for joy and harmony, not frustration or anger. You get too lazy to change and the body gets stuck in fear!

There is another way in which the body gets stuck in a rut, and that is when you are caught up in the energetic projections of others.

If you are an outlier, you are marching to the beat of a different drum. Your peer group or your community may feel so threatened by your unconventional ways, that they project their fears and negative thinking outward onto your energetic field. If your boundaries are not robust, you will find yourself sinking into their fears, and you'll start to doubt yourself and second-guess your new path forward.

This is an analogy I often use.

Let's say that you are all set to sell your house and you are excited to get it done. You tell everyone your plans, and your friends start interjecting their opinions and concerns:

Do you think that it's the right time to sell?

Maybe prices will be higher in a year, you may be missing out on the gains!

Packing is so much hard work!

Where will you go to find something as nice as this?"

Such people are doing a very good job of pushing their own fears onto you, and you absorb their doubts and negativity.

The end result is that you defer your original decision, you wait to sell your home, and you may or may not get a better price at a later time. Meanwhile, you are wallowing in uncertainty and negativity.

So how do you dig yourself out from down under? How do you step up to the plate to take bold action? There are many simple things that you can do to invite desired changes into your life.

Here's one very simple but very effective step to let go of fear.

When you wake up in the morning and before you go about your day, write down on a piece of paper what you are afraid of, and write down the answer that bubbles up in your consciousness.

Next, crumple up that piece of paper and toss it into the trash can. Follow that by saying this little prayer.

"Thank you, God, for releasing my attachment to these beliefs and for imparting in me the strength and courage to take action. Remove all forces and enemy spirits that have worked against me. Thank you, God!"

As you go throughout your day, take a simple action or two to release the fear that was earlier identified.

For example, if you have a work colleague that has deliberately made you feel small or inadequate in your job, and you feel that your job is threatened, take steps to remedy those fears. Those steps might include:

- Getting to know the person a little better and vice versa

- Developing a backup plan for your career path, like requesting a change of departments

- Opening a savings account

- Updating your resume

- Creating an environment in which you are strong enough to say, "Please do not speak to me in that way."

- Requiring that all interactions be carried out in kindness

When you take little steps, you are in fact seeing the fear for what it truly is—an exaggerated and overblown anxiety—and you will discover that you have within you the power to deal with the fear!

With that confidence, you may discover that the world is not out to get you, nor is it a scary place. It is in fact a place filled with opportunities . . . when you look up from your fears to really look and see!

Rebuilding Your Foundation

Making changes in our lives can be very overwhelming!

Remember that when you make the decision to change your life, it will take some time to undo your behaviour, or reverse an ingrained pattern of behaving in a certain way. It will take time, and you will get pushback from many people around you who will resist your transformation. That is because when you change, it triggers them. They will feel, even if it's subconsciously, that they too need to change.

There will also be moments of sadness, when you have to let go of people that you previously thought were your biggest supporters. Remember, some changes might manifest instantly but if you don't see any changes, don't be hard on yourself!

One little decision alters the trajectory of your life forever, but you have to commit to making all of the adjustments that this new life requires. In some cases, transformation becomes a way of life, always consciously tweaking what no longer works. This is how I live my life every day, making the effort to change and lay the groundwork for the new, the positive, and the wonderful to come into my life!

You must always be willing to look at things from a new perspective, to see what you can do differently. Even now, when I know that I have to make changes, I get scared to do so but during such times, I lean further into Spirit and I jump!

Here's a simple exercise to make the step forward easier.

Imagine a large piece of brown paper in front of you. Then, visualize yourself jumping through it. This exercise will remind the body that change is not a brick wall that will hurt you when you try to barrel your way through it. Many people believe change is painful, it really isn't!!

This exercise will help you to lean into the new as it is unfolding before you, so that you'll enjoy the journey so much more!

To help you rebuild your foundation, I have put together a list of simple and easy things that I like to do, and which work well in helping me transform for the better.

They are easy to do, and some steps can be undertaken immediately. All of them can make a marked difference in your life!

In this chapter, I'll talk about three of these. In the following chapter about gratitude, I'll discuss those building blocks that will strengthen your foundation for the rest of your life!

Mark your boundaries. Stay firm with them!

You need to be aware of what you can let in, and what you need to leave out. It is important in the rebuilding process to fill your physical and energetic spaces with loving and kind people, thoughts, and beliefs.

Therefore, choose to participate in those activities that uplift you, empower you, and inspire you towards hope and peace. Take up yoga or tai-chi. Join a meditation group, an artist's workshop, or a spiritual retreat. Listen to inspiring podcasts (find mine at www.tracylclark.com), go for a nature walk every day, or join a conservation-minded hiking group.

Fill your home and office with scents and fragrances that are relaxing and calming. Burn yummy scented candles. Have a nice soak in the bathtub with Epsom salts to draw out toxins. Cook a nutrient-rich meal for you and your loved ones, or just for yourself, to the sounds of healing music.

Cut the cable!

Television and news can create a lot of unnecessary fear with their focus on over-sensationalized, overdramatized bad news, and when you get too much of that, the fear ends up taking root in your mind.

Be deliberate about your choices to ensure that you have peace and quiet in your home. If you can't find a quiet spot in your home, maybe it is a good time to change things around a bit. Kids are wonderful but if you don't set aside some quiet time for yourself, they will drive you batty, and both parent and child will end up driving each other mad.

Stuck in a toxic relationship?

Is there any scope to improve the relationship?

Maybe you have pursued every possible route to better it but nothing has changed.

In rebuilding a strong foundation for your own life, you may have to recognize that the time has come to end that particular relationship!

Don't hang onto a lost relationship because you are afraid of being alone.

You are already alone if you are stuck in a dysfunctional relationship. If you have the courage to change your life and to take one step at a time, or several leaps at once, to improve your life, the Universe will support you!

It will send you more of the good things that you have in your life, including loving and kind friendships and relationships.

Toxic relationships can be so much baggage, that I address it more fully in the next chapter. For now, let me leave you with these words that I found online by an anonymous author:

"You gotta start hanging out with people who fit your future, not your history!"

Commit to inner work. Inner work is as necessary to a life of change as breathing is to living. It is only when you look closely into the triggers that prompt reactive behaviour that you can do something about it. What are some of these triggers?

Playing the victim, being the people-pleaser, hating people because everyone is out to get you. Feeling unseen, or feeling that prosperity is only for the rare elite, and not for you, are some one of the more common triggers.

To get these negative perspectives out of your life, write them down.

Bring your list of issues to a healer like me, or to a coach that you love and trust. Work towards releasing these old patterns that may have been passed down in your family from generation to generation, or that you may have picked up from the peers around you.

Be real! Don't fudge the issue or downplay its importance. If it's there and it has made your life miserable, don't rationalize why you are holding on to it. Let it go! . . . and make space for new, life-supporting patterns and behaviours to come in.

A picture says a thousand words, so how about creating a vision board?

You can make a small one or a big one. Just let your imagination go free and once you've finished your board, put it away.

Don't look at it every day! When you look at it every day, you are anchoring in the picture on the board. When you put it away you are giving it to God to create better than what you could even come up with! You've done all that you need to do to send your desire to the Universe. You can't force the pace of its manifestation, just let the Universe do its work! Maybe in a year or two, you can pull out the board and see for yourself how you've truly manifested your dreams and visions over time.

Proclaim and ask. Proclaim loudly to the God of your understanding what you want to create, then ask to be shown the next steps to bring this into your life. When you see something that you want, you can do this exercise:

Say loudly, "Thank you God! I proclaim and impart that I am going to take this and I am going to grab that for my life!" and then stand up, reach up in the air with your hand to grab the mental image of the object of your desire, and bring it back into your heart as you put your hand over your heart space.

This is a really fun exercise that I teach in my classes!

The Universe, the Source, the Creator (whatever name you have for the Divine), wants to give you everything, and all that is expected of you is to stand up and take it!

Many people feel guilty when they ask for or take things, but that shame comes from feeling unworthy or undeserving. If you feel this same guilt, you have to flush it out of you because God really wants to give you whatever you desire, and you do not want guilt standing in your way of receiving!

Ask freely! How can you get that new job? What can you do to pull that new job towards you? Asking questions like these, even quietly to yourself, will connect you to a bigger faith and the energy of love. Then always say thank you!

Do you know what the secret is to manifesting in the Law of Attraction?

It's to stay in your heart space, to really know, breathe, feel, and live as if your desire has already manifested. Trust that God has it completely and that it will show up better than you expect!

When you do this often enough, you will start to feel the energetic shift inside—the energy of creation—even before the object of your desire materializes in this dimension. I can always feel the shifts in the energetic field before I make a bold move that I desire or before abundance flows in.

It's lovely when you are so attuned to the energy of creation because it feels a little like Christmas, when you can open that special present for which you've been waiting!

Proclaim loudly as to what is your birthright! Embrace it enthusiastically and command it to come into your life, because you are ready for it, and God wants you to have it!

Keep in mind that when you begin asking questions, and start proclaiming and commanding the energy of creation, you will be tested!

If there are subconscious attitudes or beliefs that are impeding you from fully receiving what you have asked for (such as feeling underserving), the roadblocks will show up. When they do, don't think of them as a failure of creation. Instead, view them as a signal that there are inner obstacles that you have to clear out or put right.

That is the time to embark on your inner and outer work to get rid of the fears and the negative thought patterns. Be done with them and reset the mind and body!

To do this, I teach my clients a very powerful Body Regeneration technique called "One Simple Tool" that resets the heart-drive, which you can find on my YouTube channel.

When you do get these erroneous attitudes out of your system, you will feel your body getting lighter, as if unwanted baggage is being lifted from you.

Celebrate them as they surface!

Let me share a secret with you!

The more energy work that you do to restore your inner self to become more loving, more compassionate, more humble, and be more trusting . . . the younger you will start to look! Inner work naturally reverses aging because as the heaviness of the energetic baggage is removed from your body, you will no longer be weighed down by internal stresses and pressures. People will come up to you and ask for your anti-aging secrets.

God will restore the youthful blessings inside of you as the system becomes happier.

I get those questions all the time. People ask me what creams I use and what workout routines I go through. My answer is simple . . . nothing!!

All I do is make sure my energy is moving and stays light, happy, connected and at peace. The more I stay in this energetic state, the faster creation happens!

The Time Has Come to Choose

Which side of history do you want to stand on?

How do you want to be remembered when it's all said and done?

Do you want to be spoken of as the person who lived life to the hilt and who answered the call to be your most creative, prosperous, happy, and healthy self?

Or will you be described as the one who backed down from realizing your highest, deepest potential?

The time has come for you to choose!

Testimonial 7:
The Real Deal - My Life Is Truly Unrecognizable!

I have been working with Tracy for a little under two years, and my life is truly unrecognizable. She is the real deal when it comes to her gifts and abilities to support people in transforming their lives. When I started working with her, I had just relocated my son and myself to start a new chapter in life. I purchased a new home, and although looking like I had it all together, there were still some things missing.

I was intuitive and strong mentally, yet spiritually and emotionally, I needed some deep support and strengthening. I always second-guessed myself and never truly trusted my choices. Although my life was good, and I had many successes, I was still very weak in my heart and my core spiritually.

Since working with Tracy, and clearing and cleaning out old patterns, thought forms, belief systems, and so much more, today I am physically, mentally, emotionally, and spiritually fit; I am feeling so strong in my core, and getting stronger every day. My lifestyle has changed dramatically in terms of my eating habits, my exercise, my spiritual practices, my circle of friends, my career, the quality of my romantic relationship, and my stepping into my mission in life. My levels of fears have drastically diminished, and my ability to see who I am and who I choose to be has changed; I truly love who I am and who I am growing up to be.

When I look in the mirror, I like and love the person staring at me; not in a vain way, but more in a connected to spirit way. I am connected to my highest and purest light within, and every day I learn to shine it brighter and brighter. If you're ready to truly transform your life (like, no joke), look no further. Tracy and this beautiful community she has created are filled with love, compassion, support, and so much nurturing encouragement; I love being a part of something so powerful and so beautiful. Give yourself the gift of true love, and work with this beautiful and amazing angel named Tracy L Clark. Thank you Tracy, as my life is more than I could have dreamed. I love you and thank you for gifting me with the gift of true love!

– Tara Moore

Chapter 8

The Power of Gratitude and the Power of Giving

"Open your hearts to gratitude. Truly thank those on your path without whom you would not be so amazing!"

– Tracy L Clark

Gratitude changes everything!

It changes the way that we live, breathe, and act in the world, and it changes the way the world acts back to us.

When you are in a state of gratitude, you turn your attention to what's right in your world. You shift your focus to what's working, and you appreciate that which is wonderful and beautiful, from the smallest thing that you take for granted to the biggest miracles!

Let's take something simple, something so innocuous that you forget that you need it every second of your life—your breath. Have you recently expressed gratitude for your ability to breathe? Are you grateful that your body is so miraculously wired that you breathe without having to put conscious thought into it?

Breathing is a process that most of you take for granted, yet it is so indispensable to your survival that horrible things happen when you can't take your next breath.

As little as a minute after your last breath, your brain cells start to wither and die.

After three minutes, the neurons are damaged more extensively and the harm is likely irreversible.

After five minutes without taking a breath, death is imminent.

Of course there are exceptions—free divers intensively train to hold their breath for long periods of time. I am just talking about you and I, and how without the process of breathing that we take for granted, we are not able to live.

As you read the paragraph above, did you feel a spark of appreciation for who you are, and how masterfully you are designed?

Did you feel your neural pathways shifting to move you into a space of gratitude and away from your normal state, whatever your normal feeling state is?

That's what gratitude does for you! The more that you are grateful, the more you can change your life, and the faster you can do it!

I encourage you to make gratitude a part of your daily life.

Gratitude shoves aside anger, depression, and anxiety because when you are grateful, you are able to change your perception about any situation. You are filled with such positive emotions that you don't have the time, nor the space, for anything else. Gratitude helps you to bypass ego, frustration, and distraction. It draws you into the power of the moment and connects you to a bigger spiritual power!

The way in which our world is set up, we are constantly barraged by ads on television, social media, and billboards to keep buying and adding more, and to throw away that which is old and replace it with what is new.

We've become so consumed by what we don't have, and what we have yet to achieve, that we overlook the amazing miracles that have already unfolded in our lives!

Miracles come in all sorts of shapes and sizes!

They show up every day when you tap into the power of being thankful, and the power of giving and receiving.

For example, when I am driving my car or walking around my house doing errands, I say, "Thank you, God, for . . . ." and I list all of the things for which I am truly grateful. These can range from being able to get out of bed in the morning to see another day, helping clients open to life-changing miracles, having time with my children, having money in the bank to buy food, being loved by the amazing friends that I have, or being blessed to go on trips around the world to meet people from other diverse cultures!

I say thank you to the Universe for the brilliant summer day, where I can just relax in the sunshine or hit a beach to enjoy the laughter of the people around me.

Have you done that for yourself recently?

As you're waking up in the morning, before you put your feet on the ground, do you take five minutes to say a prayer of gratitude? Do you welcome the dawn, being grateful for another day to fully live your purpose? Before you go to sleep do you do the same thing? If you take these simple steps, you will watch the miracles turn up to transform your life. Remember, these are the most powerful times of the day to connect to Spirit and create from your heart-drive!

However, could the opposite be the case with you? Do you start your day with thoughts like:

"It's a little more than I want to pay"
"I hate living in this small house"
"My colleagues at work are bugging me"
"Why is he more successful than I am?"

Have you noticed that when you focus on the glass half-empty . . . tiresome colleagues, financial lack, and unhappiness with your life . . . you receive even more of that which bothers you?

It is really important that you give thanks in every area of your life!

Gratitude increases dopamine, the feel-good neurochemical, and it gets your brain wanting to do more of what you just did. In short, the more that you ARE grateful for, the more you will find to be grateful for!

You live in an interconnected world, where every action you take leads to and impacts a series of other actions. Energy flows where your attention is focused!

Therefore, if you focus on gratitude, then your brain, your subconscious, your heart, and your consciousness will inevitably direct you to choices, decisions, and actions that will lead to even more for which to be thankful!

If you are one of those people who are driven to get to the next big thing, and you don't pause to reflect on and appreciate what you have, you'll find that your happiness soon takes a bad hit!

Gratitude doesn't mean that you should aspire for more and desire more.

It means to be thankful for what you've achieved, what you've learned along the way, and what you have now that will support you to get to your next level. When you are immersed in a state of gratitude, life just seems easier, more fulfilling, and more joyful!

Gratitude is Not Just Lip Service

Yes, there are countless books and articles on gratitude, but there is a piece missing in most of these narratives!

You can offhandedly say, "I'm thankful for my dog, I'm thankful for my kids, I'm thankful for my house. Thank you, thank you, thank you"—and then carry on with your day, but if your heart is not engaged in this, what you've said is only a string of words that lack truth and potency.

When you are fully feeling gratitude from your heart—when you close your eyes, and you say with deep feeling, "I am so thankful that I live the life that I live! I am so thankful for those little things that show up every day! I am so thankful Suzy bought me lunch today!"—then that is the point in time when doors open in your life to create miracles!

I see miracles in my life every day because I live in gratitude, but miracles are not unique to me, and they don't happen just because I am connecting every day.

It is your Divine birthright to have miracles too!

Acknowledging thankfulness is the key to opening up and welcoming miracles into your life every day!

"It's a great day! I woke up today! I'm on the right side of the ground," is a joke I often said to myself. It matters greatly to me that I can get up in the morning because of all the illnesses that I have endured, and there were times in the past when I wasn't sure that I would wake up to see a new dawn. So from my heart, I would always say, "Thank you! Thank you, God, the Universe, and the Divine—thank you to the powers that be that I woke up today!"

Once, at a workshop, I conducted a gratitude exercise where I asked each person to speak from the heart about the things in life for which he or she was grateful.

When the first person spoke from her heart, all the men and women in the room started to cry. They didn't fully understand why that was happening, but when they moved into a state of gratitude, their hearts were forced open and they became clear about all that was truly wonderful in their lives!

Then we got to someone who was not able to articulate the words, "I'm grateful!"

This person copped out by saying instead, "Whatever they said," and I could see that he was dodging the exercise because his heart space was completely closed to life's blessings. He had undergone so many challenges that he couldn't find anything for which to be grateful, even though there were many when he got around to pondering it. He dwelt so much on what wasn't working that he just couldn't fathom that being alive and being at the workshop were things for which to be grateful.

As we went around the room, more tears were shed, but these were tears of love, harmony, and gratitude.

When you are in the energy of gratitude, and you are sharing that same space with other people who are also in the energy of gratitude, it's really going to change your life!

Change comes easily! If it doesn't, it is because your expressions of gratitude are not connected to your heart.

To help you start experiencing being grateful from your heart, I would like to encourage you to start a gratitude journal. On each page, write down only five to ten things for which you are truly grateful. Pen into your journal this starting line: "I am really grateful for . . . ," and fill in the blanks.

As you write, FEEL it, say it out loud, and declare that nothing will get in your way!

Write every day for at least 30 days.

I suggest 30 days because something changes within the cellular structure of the body when you do something for 30 days. It takes that length of time to fully form a new habit and to integrate the change into your body to fully form that new habit.

Commit to just five minutes a day! You can even do it at work when you are able to create five minutes of me-time for yourself.

Giving With Joy, Not Obligation

Gratitude and giving go together hand in hand. It's something that I talk about often and I get questions as to why I link them together.

Did you know that when you give generously from your heart, good things come back to you?

In the old days, a church-going congregation would be told that they had to give back to the church, and they were advised on how much they had to give. Although tithing may have started ages ago, what wasn't understood then, and is probably still not fully comprehended now, is that you should never give out of a sense of obligation!

When you give because you are expected to, in any area of your life, whether it is your money, your time, your love, or your effort, that form of giving won't attract anything new and worthwhile to you. Giving from obligation or guilt won't create miracles in your life.

I say this because when you give just because you have to, the energy of flow shuts down or is diverted elsewhere, and you become closed off to miracles.

On the other hand, when you give from your heart, you feel differently. You give because it enhances your purpose and your compassion, and because every part of you is singing, "I want to give!"

There are SO many ways to give!

You can give to your church or to your friends. You can give your time and your energy, such as baking a cake for someone, driving your friends' kids to soccer, or donating to good causes . . . without doing so reluctantly!

You can give willingly and lovingly, while saying inwardly and outwardly, "I am so happy that I can do this for you! I feel so grateful that I can do this for you!"

When you come from this space, when you give generously from your heart, more comes back to you generously!

The time for giving is NOW—not when you win the lottery, get a better job, or when you get an inheritance.

If you won't offer your time or give freely now, when you only have five dollars in your pocket, you are not going to give when you have millions of dollars in your bank account. Spirit watches you as well, to see where you give and why.

I don't second-guess giving!

When you feel it in your heart to give, even if it feels funny or awkward, GIVE!

When you give—not just your money but also your time, your energy, and of yourself—it will come back ten times or more, I see it every single day!

I get emails from people who tell me that they gave $20, and the next thing they knew, a debt of $200 had been unexpectedly forgiven!

I also hear stories from people who were prompted to give when they heard a little voice whisper, "Help this person out," and when they did, parking offences and tickets were somehow erased, or money appeared to them from an unanticipated source!

Those who gave . . . would find themselves surrounded by people willing to help and support them when they themselves needed help.

I hear these kinds of stories over and over again, and it can happen to you too, when you give unconditionally from your heart . . . with love!

You will receive the goodness you give away, and much, much more!

I am often asked if giving is similar to making a loan to someone. I never recommend lending someone money or paying for them when they are in desperation.

When you feel the need to give someone money, you do so wholly with the expectation of not getting anything in return. When you expect nothing in return for your help, something good will come back to you!

I would add that giving doesn't mean giving all the time and to everyone.

It's often been the case that I have had people wanting to pay for a session for a friend or a relative who is suffering pain and illness. Surprising to them, I say no to their offer and I explain that many times others are not ready to receive this gift, so it is like tossing your money and energy away. When I work with God, I want the person to want the shift badly, or it is a waste of time for everyone involved!

It may sound harsh, but it's often the case that the person who is sick or suffering doesn't want to spend any money on the session, even if it's not theirs, because it costs too much. In their mindset is a disbelief that the healing will work.

Although the benefactor might insist on going ahead with paying for the healing to help the person in need, I explain that the reluctance of the sick soul to accept a free healing, stems from their reluctance to make health a priority. If they did, they would find ways to give back to themselves, such as accepting the gift of a free session.

This is the way that I see it, if the friend in pain is unable to lovingly accept a gift that would be of great benefit, he or she obviously doesn't care enough for themselves to want to be restored.

People who don't love themselves enough to accept care that is freely offered to them, will stay marooned in their illness, and they will not move towards recovery, no matter what I do. There might be some positive change after a session with me, but because their negative attitude towards receiving hasn't changed, they are likely to regress.

Here's my suggestion, if you are encountering financial scarcity, if you are feeling unloved or suffering other emotional problems, if you are having a relationship glitch . . . start giving!! Give from your heart because what you focus on grows, and when you give from the heart, whatever you send out into the world comes back to you . . . multiplied!

The Power of Gratitude and the Power of Giving

To turbocharge you forward, here are two perspective-shifting practices to tap you into the power of gratitude and giving.

1. For the next 30 days, write down in your gratitude journal at least five things for which you are grateful. Ensure that you are doing so from your heart! Speak and declare them out loud, and FEEL the gratitude coursing through your body!

2. For the next 30 days, find a way to give to someone every day. It might be as simple as buying someone a coffee, giving a surprise gift, or lending a helping hand. Do so for 30 days and watch the miracles unfold in your life! Remember, a miracle is not always the big win that you want, it can be as soft and gentle as someone holding the elevator door open for you!

Sharing is Not Always Caring

"Sharing is caring" is a popular throwaway phrase these days but I take the opposite stand, I say that sharing is NOT always caring!

In a world plugged into social media, everyone wants to share a happy moment, a picture of cute cats, an opinion, or vent. There are even disruptive industries that are based on what is called "the sharing economy." Sharing is the "it" word these days.

I understand why people will want to tweet, Facebook, or Instagram something. It may be a happy moment, a new date, or the loss of a pet, and you want to celebrate or invite comfort from people whom you love but are living in far flung places. Sharing on social media means that they still get to be a part of your life.

However, I've learned on my own journey that sharing is not always caring, and that we are on the brink of being over-sharers. I am very clear about this when I work with my clients or when I teach a class.

If you take only one thing from this chapter take this, no matter where you go in your life, remember that sharing is not always caring!

Why do I say this so emphatically?

Just take a look back in your life, at a juncture when you had a new opportunity, a new job, or a new adventure in the works.

Something fabulous that lit up your soul was about to unfold for you. In your excitement, you told everyone that you came across about your good news, hoping that they would all be equally as gung-ho as you were, but what . . . in truth . . . were their reactions?

There may have been one or two cheerleaders who were happy for you, but didn't you come across the sceptics, who told you everything that could go wrong?

Didn't you get the wave of discouraging statements such as, "You aren't good enough," or "You're going to fall flat on your face and who's going to pick you up?" or "It's a pie-in-the-sky idea?" The more outrageous and out-of-the-box your new adventure is, the more likely it is that you are going to be raked over the coals by dissenters.

There is a saying: "If you want to kill your big dreams, tell them to small-minded people!"

These small-minded sceptics and doubters will project their own insecurities and risk-averse attitudes onto you. If you listen to enough of them, your self-belief starts to crumble, you second guess your decision, you question your ability to rise to the challenge, and you end up feeling so bad that you may actually reverse your assessment, and opt for a different outcome.

Ponder this for a minute, what did you feel when presented with the first opportunity? What feelings were surging inside of you before you shared the good news with others?

Did you have an inner knowing that the new path was the right path for you, and that this was the calling for which you've been waiting?

Were you gripped by a sense of having the right purpose before you shared the news with others?

Were you led off of the path because of the feelings and anxieties projected onto you by others?

One moment you were so sure of your next steps, and the next minute you were awash in self-doubt. What happened in between?

You shared and told others about your upcoming good news, and you weren't careful about with whom you shared the news. Indiscriminate sharing is not in your best interests!

It violates your responsibility to your own self-care, and it undercuts the need to protect your dreams because in the early stages, they are tender and vulnerable little things.

There may be people who will offer you a round of congratulations and loads of smiles when you tell them of your unexpected fortune, but under the guise of good-natured smiles, they may be nursing a deep jealousy or envy.

If you are totally confounded by what steps to take next, and really need a second opinion, then be discerning about the people that you pick to help you.

Make sure that they are pure in their intentions to offer help, and that they don't have a hidden agenda that may derail your dreams. Opt for the opinions of people who pick encouragement over judgement. Choose guidance from those people who have successfully walked the path that you are hoping to follow. Pick those mentors who uplift you, inspire you, and make you feel that you are capable of shooting for the stars . . . because you are!

Be mindful that the choice is yours to slow down and not immediately share good news.

Be circumspect and wait until the decision has been finalized, the contract solidified, and all the "i's" dotted and the "t's" crossed.

Your dreams, while still in gestation, are fragile and it is your right to make sure that they are adequately protected until they are robust enough to stand up to the bright lights of the world. Understand that it is completely your right to choose not to over-share and to protect your personal privacy and your sense of being!

When I decide to dive into a new creation project, I always wait until it is complete, or near completion, before I share it with the world. I like to keep my visions close and connected to God until I need further help. Quite often, when you share too soon, others can taint your visions and confuse you. Then you find it takes longer to get off the ground.

There are many things that I don't share with my family until after they are completed, because they may not fully understand my choices, and they may not be as delighted or as joyful about my decisions.

However, I have a select group of people who will celebrate my decisions with me and I am grateful for each and every one of them!

I have worked with so many people who tell me stories of their broken dreams.

Dreams that faded from lack of action and from them not having the courage to take the chance out of fear of making mistakes. Perhaps they were even dissuaded by others from chasing their so-called "pipe dream."

Mistakes are inevitable, but rather than regard them as nasty failures, view them instead as little signposts of progress because now you know how and what to do differently next time.

If you are one of those people who are holding on to dreams, no matter how old and dusty they may be, and you still want to realize them, I want to restore those dreams for you!

I want to get you to a place where they will become reality!

Life is about uplifting each other! It is about finding the people who will help you to scale the ladder of life, so that you can reach out and touch the stars, because that's what life is truly all about!

It's not about keeping your head down and getting sucked up in the endless wheel of working, hating your job, paying taxes, and getting sick!

Sure, work and taxes are integral parts of life but you can choose work that is joyful! You can choose careers that sing to you and stretch your creativity, which reward you financially, emotionally, and spiritually!

You will never be fully ready for the opportunities that come but it's more important to act in the direction of your dreams than to do nothing. Surround yourself with carefully chosen people who are in your corner, and it will be these same people in whose lives you will make a positive difference!

Simple Things to Do Right Now to Change Your Life

Change can be overwhelming! You may have opted to grow and change but how do you even start?

Deciding to change your life is a monumental step!

Acting successfully on it also requires that you make a conscious effort until new, life-enhancing, positive habits are fully in place.

You have to live the changes—breathe them, speak them, and dream about them—and when the momentum accelerates, you will find yourself happier, more successful, more productive, and more creative!

What happens when change takes more time than you expected?

Our universe is ever expanding. Everything is accelerating energetically and change seems to be the new normal. However, I have worked with clients who have told me that certain areas of their life changed rapidly, while other areas stalled, why is that so?

Here are the possibilities:

- It's not the right time for these particular changes to take place in your life.

- There may be other areas of your life that need to change first, before the next set of changes can occur.

As long as you don't give up easily, and as long as you take the required steps every day of your life, you become what you repeatedly do. You hold in your hands the shape of how your life turns out, so prioritize what is crucial for your happiness.

The more that you DO in the direction of your visions and aspirations, the more you will connect to the forces of the Universe that will open doors, and lend speed to your wings to move you forward.

In Chapter 7, I shared with you three simple practices to rebuild your foundation. In this chapter, I complete the list with six more life-changing steps.

No, you don't have to do all of them at once! Start with 2–3 each month, and commit to finishing those before starting on the next batch.

Be kind and patient with yourself! You have been in a certain groove for so long that it will take time to unravel the old patterns of being.

Some of your desired changes may come immediately, while others may take more time but whatever you do, make the changes with compassion. Don't berate yourself with anger or be suffused with guilt for taking so long to get to this stage.

Do something every day! Do more on days that you feel great and feel capable of conquering mountains. Do just one thing on days when you would rather just stay in bed.

1. Clean Out the Clutter

Get real about the things that no longer work for you. Clear these out in the same way that you would reorganize your wardrobe. You may have clothes which you no longer like, nor fit into, but they are still taking up hanging space in your closet. You rationalize not throwing them away with the excuse that "maybe the trend will return one day."

In the meantime, the only thing that these old clothes are doing is making it difficult for you to access the rest of your wardrobe, and are hindering you from bringing in new clothes that fit you better.

When patterns of behaviour, relationships, or environments no longer work for you, LET THEM GO to create the space for activities or relationships that are deeply meaningful and fulfilling.

2. Anchor into Faith

Faith means to TRUST, KNOW, and BELIEVE in something bigger, be it God, Source, Divine Energy, or even family or a worthy cause. Anchor into your faith, and do it with love!

When you do, the energies that flow to you, through you, and which guide you to act, are love, compassion, and kindness—all of the universal forces of power that spring from the Creator.

Faith doesn't require judgement, it requires belief!

We are here on earth to experience life, to learn lessons, to redress karma, to be light-workers, and to grow into our fullest potential as creative, compassionate, and loving beings. Do something every day to anchor into your faith, that which is invisible and unseen.

Faith is moving the unseen, in the field of energy, into the seen.

Don't just trust what your eyes can see because there are many, many things that they cannot see. You can't see in the dark, but that doesn't mean there is nothing in front of you! You can't see the furthest reaches of the Universe but that doesn't mean that the stars and galaxies are not there, glowing brightly!

Faith means believing in a Creative Force that is bigger than us!

3. Release Judgement

Release judgement of yourself and of others every single day!

It might be easier to do this when you recognize that everything that is happening to you right now, is a mirror of what's going on inside of you. If you find yourself judging a friend, or even a stranger, take a pause and realize that your judgment is a projection of something that you are dissatisfied or unhappy about, with yourself or your own life.

When you find yourself judging, stop and delete the judgement, and send that person love instead!

It's really a very easy exercise! Do this as often as you can remember to do so.

Sure, you are bound to forget now and again. You may even forget lots of times, but give it your best shot with this affirmation: "I am not going to judge! I am not going to judge the people that I meet today. I am going to stay open and out of judgement!"

Judgement is a dense emotion, so the more you clear it out of your system, the lighter, the clearer, and the less stressed you will feel.

My youngest daughter is a wonderful example of someone who doesn't judge others, and she gets quite upset with people who do!

The way she views it is that she doesn't know the stories behind a person's life, or what is causing the person to be rude, off-handed, or nasty. She said to me once, "I don't live in their life and I don't know their situation. I will send them love and compassion, and I will delete the judgement that I just sent to them."

I am very proud of her because young people can be harshly judgmental, and they take that mindset with them into adulthood. She lives with her heart wide open and she inspires the people who come into contact with her to do the same.

4. Create Sacred Space

Find a space for peace and quiet. Whether that is a spot for meditation, a park in which you can take daily walks, or a space where you can just relax and cook or knit.

Create daily time for yourself in that quiet place because even just 15 minutes a day will quiet the mind. When that happens, your body, your soul, and your spirit will come into alignment. Then you will connect more easily to the Universe and the Creative Force will flow through you more easily. You are already connected to pure creative energy, to your body, your heart, your brain, and your spirit, but the chatter of your mind acts as a roadblock.

When you still that endless chatter, in the quiet of your sacred space, creative energy flows through you and brings you inspiration, ideas, insights, and "ah-ha" moments.

You will sleep better, you will better recall your dreams, and miracles will happen!

That's a pretty good trade-off for just 15 minutes a day!

It's as simple as taking a bath, or walking in the rain, because connecting to the earth is a wonderful way to restore and regenerate the body and your energetic frequencies.

5. Love and Bless Your Food

Your body is 70% water, and water reacts easily to frequencies, so love and bless your food! It conveys energy and frequencies into your body and you want them to be carrying only positive vibrations. One of the teachings I really love is by Dr. Masaru Emoto. His series of books, starting with The Hidden Messages in Water, revolutionized our perceptions about how words, emotions, and intentions positively alter the shape of the water crystals. Water is sensitive to energetic frequencies—positive words carry higher level vibrations, and damaging words have lower level vibes.

There are loads of videos online about his work and I love knowing that if you bless your food, if you write uplifting words like love, thank you, and kindness onto containers with water or food, the words will raise the vibrational levels of the food.

When you eat or drink blessed food or water, the positive vibrations that they carry will transmute negative energies in your body, rejuvenate your body, restore optimal performance, and refresh your energy!

I bless my food and write love on everything that I eat and it makes the food taste better and digest more easily. Blessing your food, or speaking over what you eat and drink, is a very simple and fun tool to use in your everyday life to enhance your well-being.

I encourage you to research Dr. Emoto's work, to see how water crystals are made beautiful by elevating words, and made distorted by depressing ones.

6. Sowing

Sowing is a religious term you may hear a lot about in church.

If you are stuck in financial difficulties or want to improve your finances . . . sow!

What does sowing mean on a day-to-day basis?

It's not just about giving away money!

I believe sowing refers to a gifting of time, ideas, emotions, support, and understanding to others. Wherever you donate your time or your money, sow it in places where what you receive in return will refresh your spirit, elevate your soul, and enhance your happiness. There are many, many ways to help!

Sow into the people who uplift you and shift you. It may be your church or your energy worker. It may be a GoFundMe, volunteering for a pet rescue, helping out in shelters . . . the list is endless!

Sowing will change your entire outlook on your life. It's a simple thing! It doesn't require thousands of dollars, only the amount of money, time, or effort that is right for you. However, I have learned to listen when I hear God telling me how much to sow and where. Make sure you listen and act even if it feels off or too much.

Trust me, you will not regret it! God works in mysterious ways!

I have many souls who join one of our programs, or attend our Soul Sunday service, to better their lives. Our community sows so much back to the world, that the energy of giving comes back to bless those who participate!

Giving is a huge energy that will enhance your ability to receive, but exercise some prudence when you give. When you sow, make sure that the values of the receiving organizations align with your own. There are many organizations that don't share the benefits, and instead, hoard them for themselves.

I believe that you should be sowing in all areas of your life, but be mindful that you are sowing in fertile soil!

Let's say that you have one seed and it's a watermelon seed. If you sow your watermelon seed in the desert, it won't grow and you won't have food.

On the other hand, if you find good, lush ground in which to plant your watermelon seed, it will germinate and flourish, and it will produce lots of watermelons for you to eat.

What does that mean? It means to choose to sow in those places where you can transform people's lives and attitudes. That way they can go on to improve their lives, in turn they will positively influence others, and you will reap bountiful blessings!

There was once a gentleman to whom I wanted to gift some money. He and his family had inspired me in many areas of my life and I wanted to give them some money as an expression of gratitude. However, I kept hearing a soft whisper that told me to wait. I said to myself, "How interesting!" and since I always pay heed to my intuition, I waited.

Two days later, I received some new orders for stock that we sell, plus a few other wonderful things, and I thought to myself, "Oh, I am going to gift them even more!" but I still heard the little soft voice advising me to wait . . . So, I did!

Another 24 hours later, someone gifted me some money to thank me for helping them. It was very unexpected and lovely, and that was when the little voice said to me, "Now is the right time!"

By listening and trusting, I ended up gifting this family so much more than I had originally intended because the Universe had gifted me with the ability to do more for them. I am very grateful for that!

I love to give my time, money, and energy back to people, and to give where I know that the love and giving will come back to me tenfold, because that's how the Universe works!

If you don't have a lot of money, and you really can't find a way to help someone financially, even just the simple act of buying someone a coffee is sufficient. That person will remember your heartfelt gesture and will return gratitude to you or to someone else tenfold. Sow in rich soils, and your life will change beyond your wildest imaginings!

You have the power to shape the rest of your life in the way that you desire it to be!

The powerful tools that you have in your hands are gratitude and giving! The more that you are grateful for what you currently have, the more you will attract to yourself things for which you are grateful! When you focus on "not enough," you will get "not enough!"

When you give, unconditionally and fully from your heart, blessings and opportunities will come back to you tenfold! Don't wait to give until you have millions in the bank.

If you wait, you will never give, because giving doesn't wait for a number. It begins with an open and loving heart that wants to help because you already have so much for which to be grateful!

If you want to change your life, congratulations! . . . you are in the right place!

Start right now with the simple practices which I have recommended, don't wait until tomorrow!

You can start now by going for a 15-minute walk, or giving by helping out a friend, or writing the first line in your gratitude journal.

Change begins NOW! . . . because a new, wondrous, and joyful life is waiting for you to make the first move! Promise me that you will follow through!

We are soul sisters and brothers, and I promise to keep walking this path with you. Together, we will open the doors to greatness!

Don't forget the words that you read on these pages, because every word is imparted with the energy to invite miracles into your life, when you step forward to take action!

Testimonial 8:
The Love And Support Is Priceless!

Hi I am Laura Lee Petty.

I discovered Tracy's meet-ups 6 years ago. I was so fortunate to be one of the 1st families of her Xmas give back. I honestly was over the moon and being a single mom I was able to give my daughters and myself a wonderful Xmas. Not only that, but I have been gifted workshops and the community of earth angels even gifted me money when I was super struggling. I have NEVER in my life been part of such a supporting community!

Well, Reverend Tracy goes above and beyond for me, and for so many other people as well. The love and support is priceless!

I don't know how I would've gotten through these last 6 years without Reverend Tracy and her heart of Gold!

Tracy only listens to directions from God, so Thank-you God for speaking on my behalf when I truly need the support financially, emotionally and spiritually!

On top of all of that, Tracy's Body Regeneration has helped my journey of awakening, by clearing and dissolving old paradigms. I have taken a huge leap of faith right now.

I don't think I would've done that if I hadn't gone to Tracy's workshops, of which I have been both gifted, and have invested in myself.

I am an energy intuitive, and Reverend Tracy's Body Regeneration has enhanced my gifts. When I work on people, they say that they've never had Reiki like that, but it's really all thanks to the Body Regeneration tools which move and shift things so fast.

Also, her amazing Team who have hearts of gold, will tell it to you straight, with no sugar-coating, and are always there to give a healing hand!

I feel so blessed!

I am Blessed . . . To be a Blessing!

Laura P

Chapter 9

Radical Faith, Radical Trust

*"You will not always understand why something is happening
the way it is but keep going, because Spirit always has a plan!"*

– Tracy L Clark

You cannot see faith, neither can you touch it, but you can certainly feel it!

It courses through your veins and it gives you hope!

Faith is intangible. It has no shape, nor does it have a sound. It is sheer, raw power—limitless power with untapped potential—because with faith you can walk again, even if you are crippled. You can heal yourself, even when the doctors have written you off . . . I know!!

I understand the power of faith, it is because of faith that I am whole, strong, and able to fulfil my life's purpose to heal others. To make my life count in a world filled with uncertainty, inequity, and turbulence.

The faith that I am talking about is relentless, transformative, and radical faith!

It is not the brand of faith that you exhibit while only in church or any place of worship, which disappears when you leave the premises.

The faith that has powered my life and brought me to where I am today is catalytic and it is transformative. It breaks open your heart, it opens your eyes to unlimited possibilities, and it raises your sights so that you dare to focus on new visions and to raise yourself to new heights. I call it radical faith!

- Radical faith is unshakeable hope in action. It is the unbreakable belief that even when you fail, you owe it to yourself to try again.

- Radical faith is the fearless willingness to change what doesn't work, to get to what does!

- Radical faith is deliberately walking into an unknown future— not with fear, but with certainty that unknown helpers are right by your side and even if you fall, they'll help you dust yourself off to try again.

- Radical faith is uncompromising trust in that which you cannot see.

- Radical faith is trusting that there is something much bigger than you or me steering the ship. I call it God; you may call it something else.

- Radical faith is the foundation of radical trust.

Faith arises when you choose differently!

When something doesn't go as you've planned, don't engage in purposeless drama that over-stresses you. When you have faith, you decide to try again with sharpened focus. When life throws a curveball at you, or when you are born with the deck stacked against you like I was, you can waste away the rest of your days railing against the Universe. Alternatively, you can make the most of what you have now, and set the intention to create better for yourself!

Faith doesn't mean that you do away with the desire to change or improve.

It doesn't mean that you moan about your lot in life, play the victim, and do nothing about working on yourself or changing for the better. When life tests you a lot, it means that God feels that you can handle it, and that what you need is a little testing and a little pain in order to grow into your fullest potential. At times like these, you need to grow in mental strength, count your blessings, and take one step forward at a time, NEVER losing your focus on what you desire!

Finding Faith When Young

Faith called to me when I was a young kid. I would go to different churches with my friends, and although I never resonated with any form of religion, I was curious!

My parents never went to church, they were too busy with life's struggles, but I would board the bus that would take me to Sunday school. I used to joke that I went to Sunday school so that I would get the 25-cent doughnut that would be served on the bus.

Trust me, I did want the donut too!

I would listen to the stories in Sunday school and I would feel inexplicably better. Stories of miracles brought so much joy to me.

As a young kid, I wasn't given to figuring out why, I just soaked up the peaceful vibes. When I got into my teenage years, I stopped because I became disillusioned. All of the miracles that I heard about in church had spoken to me when I was younger but they lost their appeal when I became a teen.

During that phase of my life I couldn't figure out why, if there was a God, he would subject me to so much pain. Why did I feel so lonely and unaccepted? Why did I feel so out of place in the world in which I walked every day? Nothing made sense to me, despite my questioning about the purpose of life and whether I had a place under the sun in this world.

As a young kid, I had a sense of a bigger design and plan. I felt like an old soul in a child's body but being so young, I couldn't fully articulate what that meant.

All of that disappeared when I became a teenager. I turned to drinking and listening to loud, depressing music, to tamp down how lost and unmoored I felt.

For those of you who have felt purposeless, unmotivated, and lost because life is too tough, this might sound like a familiar refrain—pressing down the painful emotions because you lacked the tools on how to manage them.

I got married very young, in a church nonetheless, because that is what one did back then. Although I knew that it wasn't right, I went ahead with the marriage anyway.

On reflection, my concept of love, based on what was around me, was to get stuck in a dysfunctional relationship. Throughout my marriage I isolated myself from people and spent my days in tears and loneliness.

So when people spoke to me about God, I rebutted by saying that if there was a God, he/she wouldn't subject me to so much suffering and pain. I truly did not want to hear it!

Eventually, I had what I call my "come-to-Jesus" moment.

I had left my marriage and when I started to learn about energy work and medicine, I came across a wonderful mentor who opened doors for me, and got me on the path of how to heal myself.

In the early stages, I asked for proof as to how and why the body could repair itself. I needed measurable data to verify the nuts and bolts of the healing process. I was the loudest one in the room saying "Show me the science!"

Although parts of me started to repair, I knew that there was something still missing and I gravitated in the direction of spirituality by learning different modalities.

Meditation didn't work for me, science could only verify results, and spirituality was sometimes flaky—but there was a missing piece that was still eating away at me!

Eventually, I leaned towards religion but it was not organized religion, with their rules and regulations that created separation.

For example, I couldn't understand how churches could be pulling in so much money but there were so many homeless in the neighbourhood, or why churches were being closed.

I couldn't understand how we'd hear in churches that we should love thy neighbour but in the very next moment, the attendees would be backstabbing each other or fighting over different points of view.

As I looked at the different forms of religion I came to understand that I had been conditioned, by many old teachings and beliefs, that God was a man in the sky doling out punishment. The relationship to God that is pushed by organized religion, is that there is an intermediary—a priest or minister—who acts as God's emissary and forgives you.

That brand of religion is all about separation from God, and that you had to please God by following a rulebook put together by man. It's about separation from one another, and that is why throughout history, man fights in the name of religion. They fight over land and over people that they can convert. They reject those that they claim are the "other" because they call the Divine by a different name and carry out worship in vastly different rituals.

I also couldn't understand the hoarding of riches by organized religion.

Why do they need more land, more soaring spires, and more gilded gold in the ceilings of churches?

When I saw through that false creed, I realized that the answer that I was seeking was not religion—it was faith, faith in a God of pure unconditional love!

It was this faith that radically changed my life!

It infused in me the belief and trust that life could be improved, it could be better than I ever imagined . . . and that I was not alone!

It was faith that assured me that with every baby step that I took, even if it was into the unknown and full of uncertainty, I was heading towards a bigger space. A space where I could grow into a better version of myself. Faith was driving me towards a whole new world of possibilities. A world in which I no longer doubted myself, one which would wake me up to my fullest potential and be of authentic purpose to a world in need.

Through the lens of radical faith, I could see that God doesn't judge. The Divine Energy of God isn't about condemning those who make mistakes, because often the only way we learn is when we fail. It's with pain that we make gains.

Making mistakes doesn't make us bad people, if that is the only way we can learn, as long as we are willing to make changes and trust in God that all is forgiven automatically, because EVERYTHING is perfect!

Rather than punishing such people, we need to open up more around faith, and inspire them that yes, change is possible!

People like you and me love hearing stories of courage and hope against seemingly insurmountable odds because such stories motivate us. They arouse a determination and a fighting spirit to reach out for better and for more, that is how miracles are seeded!

It begins with the tiniest grain of belief that ordinary folk like you and I can change, can improve, can bounce back from failures, and can aspire to new heights and greatness!

The crutch that some people hang on to is familiarity. They keep making the same mistakes because they lack the faith that God is much bigger than you or me, and the faith that they can make different choices, and choose a different path in life.

So many people cling to what is familiar, even if it is wrong, unproductive, and dysfunctional. They will keep repeating their mistakes because they doubt the goodness in themselves. They distrust that they can be better and different, and they stay unchanged, idling in a purposeless life.

Radical faith is not about waiting to be given the chance for change. It is about you stepping forward and taking that opportunity for yourself and going for it, no matter what the rest of the world is saying to you.

It is about you heeding the inner urges of your soul and the stirrings of your heart. If that particular plan doesn't work, at least you've learned one particular way that doesn't get you to where you want to be, and you can try a different route the next time.

It's not about settling for less. In fact, faith is so radical that even if you are broken like I was, that is the way that the Universe is choosing to lead you into a more purposeful and directed future!

Faith versus Religion

Trust me when I say that it took me a long time to inject the word "God" into my conversations!

It took me a long time to clear the religious programming—my way or the highway, as proclaimed by organized religion—out of my body!

Yes, in order for you to define a sacred, potent relationship with the Divine Creator, you need to eject programming that has accumulated in your field. These are the belief systems that condone judgement and separation, and that are twinned with partisan politics.

So often, you are not even aware that such beliefs are residing in your system. Old teachings that you heard and read about, or just grew up around, naturally found their way into your body and your mind. You are so shaped by them, that you discount what is true when it is presented to you, without even knowing why.

Finally, I reconciled with this piece of myself. I came to terms with the realization that there are Holy Beings and angels, and that I could have the kind of relationship with the Divine that I desired, not one that was enforced on me or prescribed by a rulebook.

The Christ Consciousness is a lovely, beautiful, and expansive energy that is available to everyone . . . but who made Christ into an exclusive club?

If the stories about Jesus are true, he didn't judge, nor did he discriminate against the poor and the sick when he was healing. He walked on this planet to awaken our consciousness and to give us hope, love and glory!

Organized religion made Jesus a member of an exclusive club, and that is why so many people have left institutional religion altogether. They have turned towards spirituality, or classify themselves as not identifying with any particularly faith.

However you label it, Christ Consciousness, God Consciousness, or the Consciousness of Oneness, it is all about compassion, humility, and of being in service to others!

In contrast, the spirit of organized religion keeps you in a box, limited and locked up!

When I became clear about my relationship to God and how it was a creative, bold, and transformative energy that brought about new hope, possibility, miracles and renewal, I said to it, "Use me, I want more of you! Expand me as a vessel so that I can serve!"

You can have a relationship with God ANYWHERE, it doesn't have to be between the pews of a church!

In fact, it shouldn't be confined to the four walls of a place of worship and disconnected from the rest of the world. Transformative faith insists that you be out in the world, changing people's lives by offering them the gift of your service.

You can . . . and I love the fact that you can . . . have this relationship with God every second of every minute of your life, no matter where you are!

Churches are great for meeting friends, finding support, and uplifting you, IF you are allowed to be the full expression of who you truly are!

You can say to God, "I realize that I messed up but I am going to do better from now on. I am going to attract the right people, and I am going to do something that I have never done before. I am trusting that I will be guided when I take the next step. I am watching for the signs that God places in front of me to take action on them!"

With all that being said, what do I believe about sowing and tithing?

I believe in the principle, but I argue that tithing is not about pledging to every religious organization of which you are part. Sowing and tithing is really about showing up where you are.

It is about supporting those who support and lift you up. It may be a speaker, a coach, or a church that you decide to support. YOU decide how much and why!

Give WILLINGLY, I cannot stress the importance of this enough, to receive! This has always rung true!

You receive huge blessings when you are grateful that all of your needs are provided for. When you come from faith, you know that tithing is a way of giving back or paying forward through acts of love and connection, such as when you pay for the person in the checkout line or buy a stranger a cup of coffee.

I cannot repeat it enough that the God Consciousness DOES NOT PUNISH!

I want to go back here for a minute because I want to be clear.

I also thought that my health problems and the traumas that I had lived through were a form of retribution because I wasn't being good enough, or perhaps because I did something wrong and was not aware of my errors.

However, each time in my past, just before I was going to die or check out, something came in to reverse that decision. It was inexplicable but this rejuvenating energy lifted me out of the gloom that I was in.

Years later, I realized that it was Spirit coming through to help me remove the dark, negative energy that was dragging me down, and lift me up to the Light! It wasn't easy to come back to the land of the living when I had already left my body.

I realized that God was lifting me up and all of that trauma became my biggest gift in how I serve today!

There was always a lot of pain in the recovery, and I had to dig deep and hold on to my faith like a lifeline . . . but I did!

So often, you may feel like you are being punished for something that you did and you get sick as a result. There is nothing further from the truth!

You are not being punished, it is something that you are here to go through.

During such times, lean in more to God, and lean into your faith!

Remember that even if your body is not well, like mine used to be, speak to your body, thank God for your healthy body, and believe that you are being repaired!

Believe it, so that you can plant the seed with God and see it flower!

Do you want to hear something amazing?

I am here today writing this book, speaking to all of you and using my vessel as a channel to serve God with my healing hands, precisely because I held on tightly to the unwavering belief that something good and better was in store for me. My radical faith assured me that I was capable of a whole lot more, and that I could serve in bold ways that I wasn't even aware of yet!

Faith is about hope, humility, love, forgiveness and connection. THAT, to me, is the true definition of GOD! There is no punishment in faith because God doesn't punish!

God puts lessons in your way for you to grow, change, and discard those bits of yourself that no longer work, so that you can develop into the best version of yourself and be of service to the world in which you live. When you have faith, you are thankful for the gift of life that you have been given, and you make the most of your time on this earth!

Keep taking action, keep moving, and keep talking positively to your body that you know that there is something better!

Look out for the signs, because the God Consciousness will send you signs to guide you in the right direction, or gently nudge you back when you stray away from the right path for you.

In the early days of my business, there would be negative opinions and judgements about me stepping into my gifts and my decision to work with my healing hands to carry out the energy work with God. On bad days, when I felt like maybe there was something else in store for me, I would play this game called "Give Me a Sign!"

Well, the very next day there would be three or four emails in my inbox from clients thanking me for changing their lives for the better, and expressing sincere gratitude for my help. Those emails were definitely a sign that I was in the right place!

When I received these signs, I would release any frustrations, anger, and disbelief.

I would thank God for sending me the signals because when I was in gratitude, I moved forward with more hope, more strength, and more grace.

God/the Universe would hear my plea and answer me immediately!

God gave me a gift to be a vessel to help many learn how to connect with their inner gifts, to help souls to heal and repair their own broken lives, and to help guide them on their troubled paths.

The way that my life was, it was hard for me to NOT be mad at God, or to not hate my life! My life was designed so that I could learn, it was my Earth School.

I had to go through such training so that I could help many souls.

Never, ever underestimate or think badly of your training at Earth School, because the curriculum is designed for you for a specific reason!

I have encountered souls who believe that even if you have a God-given gift, you are not to be rewarded for it, and such a gift can only be used within the church.

This is an old, outmoded set of beliefs!

You are gifted, I am gifted—we are ALL gifted and talented in our own ways—and GOD does not want anyone to starve or be poor!

Such worn-out belief structures are man-made, not God-made! Those are the ideas of men, not ideas from God.

Never forget, poverty does NOT come from God! Poverty stems from old, man-made beliefs to keep you stuck!

We evolve as humans when we believe that there is a bigger, loving, compassionate presence out there, with whom you develop a relationship of your own making.

I know, without a shadow of a doubt, that this presence is guiding us each and every day and that what we are asking for is already done!

It is manifesting the moment that we ask and it is being watered and nurtured into fruition. Our job is to keep going on that path!

These blessings may not manifest on our time frame, the time frame that is shaped by ego, and sometimes they don't manifest at all . . . at least not in the shape that we expect! Rather than get crestfallen and daunted when that happens, shout out with optimism and confidence. Say "Thank you, God" when your best-laid plans and intentions turn out differently, because the Universal God energy knows the perfect plan for you!

You have to believe that what you've asked for is being done in the best way for you, and that it's there, making its way from the unseen realms into your reality!

Look within, hold on to your faith, lean into the God of your understanding, and trust that everything that is unfolding is bringing you into the Light. It's this loving acceptance and unshakeable conviction that truly transforms you!

I have an acronym for this: CDC.

No, it's not the Centre for Disease Control, although in a manner of speaking it sort of describes the Body Regeneration Method™ that I founded, because when you carry out my healing work, you are connecting with your body. Your body is the centre that at some level created the sickness, and it is the very same centre that will carry out the healing!

Nevertheless, my acronym . . . CDC . . . stands for Connection, Dedication, and Commitment. With CDC, you keep going even when you think that you have no more strength!

It's like a tired swimmer, who is failing in energy and is just ten feet from the shore. This swimmer, when he or she sees the coastline, will dig deep and find those last few breaths and spurts of energy that gets him or her to safety.

Make the Choice!

Isn't it wonderful that you get to make a choice every single day of your life?

It is in the deciding, and the choice that you make, that the miracles unfold and the limitations fall off.

Choose differently, and choose better! When things don't quite pan out exactly as you hope, choose to change the way that you think, and be grateful for whatever has happened!

TRUST that the God Consciousness, which has created worlds and galaxies, has a plan and that all you need to do is to trust that the plan unfolds at the right time and place for you!

I don't play the "Give Me a Sign" game very often these days, but if you want some help at the beginning of your journey, go ahead and ask for signs!

This relationship to the God Consciousness is yours and yours alone! It is sacred to you, no one else!

No one should tell you how you shape your connection to God—not me, not your best friend, not your partner . . . NO ONE!

I may have lived through some very difficult circumstances, but those were meant to shape me to be what I am today, a healer and a guide. To point out certain truths to encourage you to open your mind, your heart, and your life, to boundless opportunities!

I was born with many physical issues, and many times I was given slim odds of moving forward in life. I went through physical trauma, emotional trauma, a broken marriage, and I nearly checked out a number of times. If I thought that this was all that God had in store for me, it was because I was told that life was hard and due to that belief, I was disconnected from the truth of what God was trying to show me!

God is already inside of you and all around you! Make God your best friend, and learn from the lessons that you have to master. Keep learning and taking action when something new shows up, and watch the blessings unfold in your life!

You are blessed to be a blessing—never forget it! FEEL it, embrace it, and know it on every level and every layer of your being!

Now God uses me as a vessel to heal with my hands, my voice, and my words.

God has been speaking to you, waking you up, gently nudging you, and showing you the signs!

Declare with me right now:

"It is my birthright to live in overflow in all areas of my life!"

Take that energy, which is awakening and stirring inside of you, and never forget what it feels like!

Do not second-guess and do not allow others to hold you back!

Walk with God/the Universe, and TRUST that you are here to unleash the amazing possibilities within!

Believe that you shall receive!

Like a candle shines brighter when there is darkness around, let your candle shine so brightly that it brings Light to whomever you touch!

Testimonial 9:
I Found The Courage To Let Spirit Take Over!

Hello Tracy,

I want to thank you jubilantly for all the work you did on me today. I watched the video this morning and listened to what you said about my request, and then I went to work. Today I was interpreting the story of a historical Catholic Mission. At around 11:00 or something I suddenly realized that every symptom I mentioned to you is pretty well gone. I swallowed about 3 times to make sure, and it hasn't come back. I know you are a worker of miracles, and I have heard many testimonials, but this was a very dear experience for me. Last night, I also found the courage to let spirit take over. As I've been working on myself energetically I've been trying to figure out how to get the results I want. I realized that to some point I have kept myself from truthfully asking for what I want because I had to figure out the details first. Spirit reminded my job is only to ask and do what spirit tells me, and leave the details to God. I was also reminded to use positive words instead of negative words when putting a request in God's hands. All of this helped me open up to the flow of blessings, and I was in a state of joy as you were working on me today. You probably knew that, but I really appreciate the amazing testimony I now have of God expressing his will through your work and how connected you are to Him. It is very admirable. I also am starting to gradually see the fulfillment of my goal, connecting to God. I know that one of your objectives is to teach us how to do this work for ourselves. I feel more confident and aware of the wonderful blessings flowing into my life that can help me connect to God in my own way as you have done.

I also wanted to thank-you for answering my request to somehow attend your weekend workshop. I didn't tell anyone about this, but I asked God to make it possible for me to learn the information that you would be presenting at this event so I could learn the action steps. Your generous offer, of gifting me the event, is an answer to this prayer and the financial miracles that I have been opening up to. Thank-you for your generosity!

Sincerely and with ever-new joy,

Michael Callander

Chapter 10

Follow the Energy

"What did you find in your closet that you are ready to let go of . . . FOR REAL? What fears are brought up that really, in truth, need to go into the bin . . . Ask yourself, are they worth hanging onto for the rest of your life, when all they do is impede you from fulfilling your dreams and mission?"

— Tracy L Clark

Let me tell you a story.

I recounted this particular narrative once in a workshop. Everyone present broke down in tears and said almost unanimously, "Oh, my God! I get it!"

I am sharing this story with you so that you'll grasp the secret behind it.

Once you do, you'll move forward in your life with clarity and conviction, and open doors to a future that exceeds every expectation that you may now have!

The title of the story is "Follow the Energy." You may have come across brief mentions of this story in earlier chapters in the book, but this is where it all comes together.

I love my parents very much. It may not sound like that is the case because of the experiences and challenges that I have gone through with them.

You may recall that my father moved a woman into our house while my mom was away visiting her family in Europe. When she came back and saw that another woman had taken her place in what used to be her house, she took my sister and me out of the only home that we knew.

This was the beginning of my fear of abandonment, which would rear its ugly head in my life over and over again!

It was only when I learned to follow the energy—the energetic footprints— back into my past, that I made a startling discovery!

I had all of these imprints of ideas, thoughts, and implants of information and perceptions stored in my body . . . and they all spoke of abandonment!

Looking back, I realized that I would attract people that would abandon me, and I would attract people that would want to do things with me and not follow up.

Where did the feeling of abandonment come from?

It had its birth pangs on that lonely sad night on the bus going from what was my safe space, to a strange, unknown city. I didn't have anything familiar with me—none of my toys, only a few pieces of clothing—and in the despair and rootlessness that followed, my tiny young body picked up a message that I was not loved by men. In this case, men were represented by my father.

The following beliefs took hold in me:

- "Men will kick me out!"

- "I am disposable!"

- "I can be thrown out at any time!"

- "The world is not a safe place!"

- Etc.

All of these perceptions had woven themselves into the depth of my consciousness, and had become a part of the pattern of who I was to become. It didn't stop there!

I was also picking up a whole lot of baggage from my mother who, in an instant, had lost her husband, her marriage, her own home, and was barely holding it together.

She was besieged by anger, fear, and worry, both emotionally and with her finances. She had left with little, besides what was in her handbag, and we ended up on welfare.

As a very sensitive child, that kind of worry and frustration seeped into my body and became my reality. I was too young to know any differently, but I was absorbing the negative emotions that were circling around me.

Throughout my life, until I came to understand how to follow the energy, I carried this programming. It acted like a special mental filter which attracted, and only allowed in, real life experiences that confirmed my negative bias and fear around men, money, and abandonment.

Peeling off the Layers

When I learned to follow the energetic pathways in my transformation, I came to understand that you slough off these imprints in layers, like the layers of an onion.

You can do this too!

Think about the recurrent issues in your life, be it abandonment, anxiety over the future or over money, the inability to get along with people, or a lack of self-worth.

Whatever it is, if you unwind the energetic threads into the past, you can pinpoint precisely when those fears were first seeded in your body.

With that new understanding, you can back these imprints out of your body, clean out the patterning from your central nervous system, and put in their spaces new programming that brings in peace and joy.

When I pulled on my energetic threads, I followed the pathway back to that night when I had my first brush with abandonment, and the consequences that followed.

As I reviewed those circumstances of my past, mindfully and consciously, I came to recognize that my parents did the best that they could at that time.

I made a decision, deliberately and in full awareness, to unconditionally forgive them and I sent them unconditional love!

I then forgave myself and thanked the Hand of God for unconditional love and justice for all, without judgement, in the way that only God knows how!

It is very important to your own healing process to have unconditional love and forgiveness, because they are the major keys to letting go of the past. It's only when you let go of the past that you can move smoothly and fully into your now, and make conscious decisions that benefit you and create pathways to a future that exceeds all of your hopes and dreams. Remember, when you give it back to God with unconditional love, the energy becomes broken.

Then you are free! . . . and so is everyone else involved!

I released any anger, confusion, or reactive behaviour that was shaped by those old patterns so that I could evolve. I made peace with the past, and when I did so, I could look at it objectively and let it go!

Do this yourself!!

When you are reconciled with your past and you let it stay where it needs to be, in the past, you will get a sense of peace. You may have previously been angry when you recounted that particular episode in your life but in releasing it, you also let go of your frustrations and your despair.

Even More Layers to Go

Despite me stepping back, following the threads, letting go and forgiving, abandonment still showed up in my life. When it did, I came to understand that I needed to peel off even more layers.

That episode with my parents was only one facet of my fears around abandonment. There was more that I needed to dive into, and I had to get on with it in order to reclaim my life and remake it in the way that I wanted.

When I worked with my teacher Olga on further delving into my layers, she asked me what had happened to me when I was between 4 ½ to 5 years old. I described the kidnapping which involved me, my sister, and my friend. She said, "That's very traumatic, I don't need to know any more!"

I replied, "Yes it was, but I feel that I have worked through the trauma."

She answered that even though I felt that I had worked through the ordeal, there was another piece that had yet to be resolved. Her advice to me was to stay open to this and the unaddressed fear would surface. I would recognize it for what it was when it did come up for air.

I finished my session with her musing to myself that the revelation was very interesting!

I made my way home, wondering what was to come forward.

My two daughters were at play and my younger daughter Christina was jumping on the trampoline. Out of the blue, without preamble or warning, she said, "Mommy, I know that you don't like us going to the park by ourselves because when you were little, you had a very bad experience." She continued, "I'm curious, I want to know how Grandma and Grandpa handled it."

My parents didn't have any coping skills, they were of a generation and an age when nasty events were buried in the closet, and were never to be given voice.

However, even though I was young, I understood. As such, I held no anger towards them because I saw that they did the best that they could with what they knew.

I looked at my daughter and said, "They did nothing! They just stuffed me in my room, let me cry, and pretended nothing happened. I cried myself to sleep, night, after night, after night!"

As I was answering my daughter's question, a light bulb came on in my head . . . this was where the last piece of my abandonment issue resided! Although I felt that my parents had done their best by me, being as sensitive as I was, I was resentful that my parents did not step up to give me the care and the attention that I required. I had no idea it was still sitting in my system!

No matter how you cut it, the kidnapping was a nightmare! The fears that ran through my body, and the tears that flowed down the cheeks of five-year-old me, were never addressed. The kidnapping was never, ever, talked about! It was never discussed by the family. Instead, it was pushed under the rug, as if it never happened.

By speaking it out loud, I found myself letting go of another layer of abandonment.

I released the resentment and anger which I had buried so deeply, and wasn't even aware that they were still shaping my life.

When you are excavating the repressed parts of you and are following the energy, ask yourself this question:

"Where in my past did I first feel this, and where has it cropped up over and over again?"

The feeling is your GPS to freedom! It is the "X marks the spot" where treasure is buried.

It is a treasure because when you can identify the origin of the feeling, you can forgive yourself, the people involved in the experience, and you can finally become free!

Choosing to Forgive

Five years into my healing journey, I went to the doctor and said "I am here because there are some bad cells in my cervix." I use the term "bad cells" to describe the C word because naming it gives it too much power!

Befuddled, the doctor asked me "How could you possibly know this?!"

I explained that I knew that it was there, and that it was a result of residual anger with my ex-husband. You can imagine the look of confusion on her face!

However, she had seen enough restoration in my body over the years to keep an open mind. The doctor performed the test and the results came back positive for the C word.

I asked my doctor to respect my desire to deal with the situation from a non-traditional approach. WE both agreed to the parameters that we would follow together, and tests to ensure that I was moving in the right direction.

I am not anti-medical, as I believe we need to work together. However, by this time I had seen my body do miraculous things, which the medical community had told me were impossible!

I then . . . at all costs! . . . worked to energetically release the final piece of anger towards my ex-husband, and forgive him for what he had done to me.

WE blame others for what they have done to us . . . but we forget that it is us who made the choices! Therefore, the anger is not at them, but within us!

When I forgave him, the anger released! Months later I was retested and to my Doctor's surprise, the test was completely clean. There was no sign of bad cells left!

Forgiveness is a hard concept to grasp and it is a sticking point that keeps many locked in a loop of anger, resentment, and victimhood. To most people, forgiveness means that they must absolve the other person of their wrong doing, abusive behaviour, or mistreatment. This mainstream concept of forgiveness is difficult to swallow.

We have been taught that if the offending person apologizes, acknowledges their wrong doing, admits that they had treated you poorly or violated you, then you would be able to move forward. This is simply not the case!

The imbedded deep rooted trauma and patterns that have etched their mark within your system do not miraculously disappear with an "I'm sorry." The apology does not remove the root and the seed of the trauma.

What if I offered you a different perspective on forgiveness?

I teach my clients that you forgive someone for YOU . . . not for THEM!

Make no mistake, forgiveness does not absolve the other person of their actions . . . but it releases YOU from holding on to deeply held emotions, such as anger and resentment, about the person or situation.

I have had several workshop participants ask me the following question:

"Sure, I can work with following the energy, but once I hone in on the point of origin, am I going to be able to forgive the people who were involved?"

Are you able to forgive?

Are you able to offer unconditional love and forgiveness to the people who might have harmed, ignored, bullied, ostracized, or abandoned you?

My answer is simple. Yes, you can!

Yes, you MUST! . . . If you want to be free!

There is great value in forgiveness! It wipes the slate clean so that you can step forward, away from darkness and into the light!

Here is a simple way of looking at it:

Your life has been influenced by the aftermath of the unpleasant experience, and you may have even replayed it over and over again in your mind. You have relived the pain and the torment as if they were fresh and real, but what about the other participants of the experience— the people who caused you harm, or the person who failed you?

Are they reliving the past encounter as deeply and as often as you are?

Probably not!

That person has gone on with his or her life and has their own issues to deal with, and in all likelihood, doesn't remember or doesn't care about what's going on with your life.

They may also have a totally different perception than you do regarding the situation.

Your life is your own! You are the only person responsible for how you create your life, and YOU are the ONLY person who can take on the responsibility for releasing the guilt, or the blame, or the demons that lurk within you!

When you take the time to pause and follow the feelings objectively, as if you are a bystander, and not get all roiled up in the tide of emotions, the sting of the negative feelings will lessen and diminish. In their place will come love, acceptance, and forgiveness!

Once you let go of the torment, you will see light coming into your field—the God-Consciousness flowing in to fill up the newly emptied space in you—to help you shift positively forward.

You may be saying to yourself right now that this is all very well and good, and you are ready to get going, but how and where do you start?

Here are some easy steps:

- Identify a feeling or negative state that you are done holding on to and wish to purge out of your field.

- Ask yourself, "Where in my past did I feel this? Truthfully, who made me feel this way?

- Dig deep . . . as deeply as you can!

- Write down notes, sketch a trail, do a mind map—do anything that helps you to follow the energetic trail back to its origin.

- Remember, everyone showed up exactly how you asked them to in order for you to grow in some way.

Once you have fully identified the source of the pain, and the people who have hurt you, let the experience go! Forgive unconditionally, and love without expecting something back! You're not necessarily forgiving the experience, and you may never get closure with the people who you feel have done you wrong. Instead, you are forgiving to stop playing the victim card, and you are forgiving to take responsibility for your own happiness!

There is a famous quote "Anger is like swallowing poison and hoping your enemy will die".

IN TRUTH! . . . .Where in your life have you held on to resentment and anger?

If you have difficulty letting go, you are holding on to the pain for a reason. Ask yourself why you are holding on.

What benefit are you getting out of it?

It might be a fear of moving forward because you've grown so used to being sheltered.

It might be a fear of loneliness because you're afraid of leaving behind what is comfortable, even though it is not self-supporting.

You may be afraid of not being able to match up to your new expectations.

By grasping onto anger, hate, resentment, or victimization, consciously or even subconsciously, you are pre-paving your road forward to be filled with those very same feelings that you are holding on to—anger, hate, resentment, or victimization.

No matter how you feel or what you feel, the feelings and thoughts that you hold are what you use—your raw materials in a manner of speaking—to create your future pathways.

By letting go of these old hates and resentment, you are creating space for new, wonderful, people and experiences to come in. You are creating space for life to come in!

Have the courage to plumb every layer of who you are, and you'll find freedom!

New, fresh, creative energy will show up to spur you forward in the direction of your dreams and visions!

It's your birthright to live fully, happily, and creatively . . . so seize it!

Follow the Energy

Follow the energy with everything that you have! Remember that everything comes down to fear or love. What are you choosing and why?

When you can truly answer this question, forgiveness becomes easy!

As you unwind your memories, say this prayer aloud or to yourself:

> "Thank you, God.
>
> I let that go NOW and send them back to you for justice and unconditional love!
>
> I release that issue to you God now, with unconditional love and forgiveness.
>
> I am a child of God.
>
> I release that issue to you, with unconditional love and forgiveness.
>
> I am a child of God.
>
> I release that issue to you, with unconditional love and forgiveness.
>
> I am child of God.
>
> Amen"

I came to realize that the only one who was holding onto my fear of abandonment, the only one who was feeding it and giving it fuel by replaying my past . . . was me!

I made a choice . . . .and you can too!
Let it go!!
Become free!!!
I commanded in a new word:
FREEDOM!!!

Once you've come to the end of your dysfunctional story and decide to let go of the past, choose a word that describes your new path. Choose a word that fills your soul!

Mine is "Freedom!" Yours can be anything that you want:

Passion
Laughter
Lightness
Creativity
Mindfulness
It can be anything!
It's your life!

Embrace it on every level and every layer, from the top of your head to the souls of your feet!

FEEL THE "NEW" DRIPPING INTO YOUR BODY! FEEL THE "NEW" EXPANDING NOW!

DECLARE:

> *"I NOW ACCEPT MY TRANSFORMATION FOR MY HIGHEST AND BEST GOOD. THANK YOU GOD!"*

Testimonial 10:
I Showed Up For Myself At All Cost!

Five years after doing my work consistently, the "bad cells" showed up.

This was totally unexpected and caught me off guard. Tracy and her Community were very supportive and stood by me throughout the process. Tracy directed me via an integrated approach, with no judgements, and explained to me exactly how and why this showed up in my life.

The scar tissue exercise on Saturday was great. I did a one year follow up after my surgery today, and the first thing the doctor said was, "You look good!"

After the checkup, he said "You have healed very well, there is no scar tissue and everything is great!"

While sitting in the waiting room, I reflected that it was seven years, on Sept 30th, that I sold the home and moved out of the toxic environment. The dates coincide with my surgery last year. Then Kelly Clarkson's song came on, "What doesn't kill you make you stronger"

Thanks to everyone in the Community that stood with me and went through this with me! There is only one more step later this month, and I know that it will be fine.

Last but not least, I also want to thank Tracy L Clark, who helped me to find out what lesson this was for me and I absolutely get it!

I showed up for myself at all cost and I made that promise to myself last year. Thanking God!

Jenn Mclaughlin

Chapter 11

The Force

"It's an energy field created by all living things. It surrounds us and penetrates us. It binds the galaxy together!"

– Obi-wan Kenobi

All life is infused with the Force—from the oldest tree to the largest mammal . . . to you! From the smallest blade of glass to the tiniest of animals and insects, including the pesky mosquito—the Force runs through everything! This Force creates everything—the air that you breathe, the rain that falls, and the food that you eat.

It creates your dreams and your visions!

The Force flows within you, and outside of you! It permeates everything and it creates everything, including this book that you hold in your hands. It is a beautiful, beautiful energy of light that brings you miracles and blessings! It gives you the strength to break through limitations, and the delicacy and grace to care for the welfare of others!

Yet you may ask yourself, if this Force is so wonderful and powerful, why is your life down in the dumps? Why isn't the Force making it better?

The answer is simple . . . it's up to you!

It's up to you whether you allow the Force to flourish in your life because every day, at every moment, you get to make a choice. You get to choose the Light or the Dark because that is part and parcel of free will.

Life powered by the Force is a life filled with gratitude for big and small joys!

It's filled with harmony and balance because you see the good in everything, including adversity. The Force gives you the confidence to climb mountains and to walk the path of the unknown. It gives you the guts to take the next step, and the one after that, because it's in walking the path that you gain in courage!

If you are not sure if you are on the side of Light, or the side of Dark, here are some points of guidance:

- When there is chaos swirling around you, when values are overturned, and hate and anger prevail . . . it is easy to give in to the dark.

- When you stop believing in your own sense of self-worth, you are giving in to the dark.

- When you feel that you have to take from someone else because there isn't enough, the dark is getting the better of you.

- When you lose all hope of a future brighter than the one you are in now, the dark is sitting within you.

- When you speak negative words into your life, you are thinking dark thoughts of yourself.

- When you are unable to forgive, you are in the dark!

The Force

When there is light, there is often dark, and these dark forces will keep you in pain, suffering, poverty, lack, illness, and hopelessness.

I say to you, DON'T fear the dark! . . . and don't be ashamed that you are vulnerable to the pull of the dark forces!

The dark has a divine purpose! It is to help you to remember that one of the highest gifts that the Divine has given you, is a reminder of who you are!

You may feel as if you are waging a battle, and it may feel like tough love to have to break through darkness to find the light . . . but it is not!

If it is difficult, it's because you have forgotten that everything that you do is of your own choosing!

Even if you feel surrounded by the dark right now but you are determined to stand on the side of the light, and you keep choosing the light, the light will break through the clouds! It will be bright and life-enhancing again!

Remember, the dark will always tempt you, but you must be aware and choose the light!

When the doctors told me that I was stuck with my neurological disorders, and the accompanying pain, they had effectively written me off. Their diagnosis pierced my heart and I could have just surrendered to their opinion and lived a sub-optimal life.

It's very easy and very tempting to give in to the dark, especially if you have been fighting for a long time. The fatigue gets to you and the lack of results erode your faith.

I could have accepted what they said and just laid down to die, but I refused to be consigned to a life of pain and I searched for a solution.

It took me years, but at the crossroads where there were two paths before me—one towards darkness, and the other towards the light—I chose to believe in the Force of good, and that beautiful, beautiful, light energy of the God Force healed me!

Have you heard the story of the bumblebee?

The bumblebee, according to science, should not be able to fly because it's just not built for flight. According to the principles of flight, it's little wings are too slight to lift its fat body off the ground, so it should only be able to walk.

It's just as well that the bee can't understand our limited concepts! The bee is created by God! It flies because it has a job to do, and it flies to carry out that divine purpose. It doesn't stop flying just because man says so. "Be the Bee . . . BE the Bee!!" Fly even when you are told that you cannot!

Remember, supernatural is within you, the Force is supernatural and you just need to believe in it and choose it for yourself!

Trust me, it wasn't easy for me, and nor will I tell you that it will be easy for you.

Here is a truth: your choice to choose the light will change the shape of your reality every step of the way!

When you visibly, truly, and faithfully choose the Force, when you choose the God-consciousness, when you opt for love, and when you vote for compassion, that is another step that you take towards the Light!

What are the benefits of falling on the side of the God Light?

- You'll move to joy, happiness, and peace, from despair, gloom, and dejection.

- You'll enjoy the support of friends, lovers, partners, and community, instead of dwelling in a solitary life and loneliness.

- You'll be blessed with inner and outer wealth, instead of fighting with greed, lack, and scarcity every day.

- You'll find doors opening to unexpected life-expanding opportunities, rather than manipulating others to get ahead.

- You'll step forward and live with certainty and clarity, guided by your inner wisdom, rather than stewing in distrust and seeking to always control.

Darkness is Seductive

There will be times when the dark seduces you.

During those times, you may believe it is easier to give in to anger, lash out in revenge, or stew in hate . . . but it wins only if you let it!

It may feel easier to choose the dark than the light, but that is a delusion!

Every time you choose the light, you will be challenged . . . but hang on tightly to the light, and the challenges will fade away!

Let me assure you of this: when the darkness threatens, you have a powerful weapon with which to fight it!

You breathe in, you stand or sit still, and you tell yourself: I choose the light!

The choice is always yours, it cannot be taken away from you—not now, not ever!

By now you know that I regard Yoda as my hero.

God works in mysterious ways!

Yoda may be a green-skinned, rubber puppet but he is an icon because he believed, without a shadow of a doubt, that the Force ran deep within him. He didn't question it and he didn't ask for scientific manuals to prove its existence.

Instead, he FELT it, he BELIEVED it, he LIVED it . . . and he raised X-wing fighters with the shake of a little green hand!

Over the years, many of us have quoted Yoda's infinitely wise quotes. Here are some of my favourites:

"Luminous beings are we, not this crude matter."

"Size matters not! Look at me, judge me by my size, do you?"

"Always with you what cannot be done. Hear you nothing I say . . . you must unlearn what you have learned . . . Try not! Do . . . .or do not. There is no try!"

The Force, which creates universes and stars, lives deep within you. It lives within the essence of your soul and if you wonder what it feels like, think about how you feel when you are in love.

When you're in love, the world looks beautiful, you shrug off obstacles, and you walk as if on air. That is how you feel when you live aligned with the Force—in love with everything in your life, exactly as it is!

Harness this beautiful energy; harness the God Consciousness!

The Force

You already have it within you!

When you choose, you are waking it up, and it becomes as bright as a lighthouse to shine the way for others!

Take the Force into the world!

Create miraculous adventures and miraculous healings!

Find new joy, wonderful people, and peak experiences!

When you live by the Force, every day becomes a bigger blessing!

The next day becomes an even bigger blessing, and so it snowballs to a joyous, sparkling future!

You feed your body with food—three, four, or five times a day. How about feeding your spiritual body more frequently than you feed your physical body?

Most people will give the spiritual body a snack once a month. You may attend a service or go to a meditation, but that is just lip service, it's not adequate nourishment for your spiritual body!

Every day, be in gratitude all day long!

Thank the God of your understanding for the blessings and the joy!

Give thanks for new doors to open!

Keep feeding your spirit body any way that you can, every second of every minute!

Thank everyone who showed up in your life to make you so amazing!

I thank my family, my kids, their dad, and my friends!

I am so grateful for each of their roles that helped to shape me into who I am today!

Allow that life force energy to keep increasing inside of you!

Never stop BELIEVING! Never stop KNOWING! Never stop TRUSTING!

There are people out there that you are here to serve!

When you are grateful for how precious your life is, and how it will matter to the world in a way that you never thought possible, miracles and blessings come to you, unbidden!

What will you choose today?

I ask you to choose wisely, love deeply, and trust with every fibre of your being that you are not alone!

God is here guiding you, working with you and through you!

You are here for a reason and it is up to you to keep changing the season that you walk through.

NEVER doubt! . . . .because I know that you are here for greatness!

God has your back . . . ALWAYS!

NOW DECLARE IT, CLAIM IT, AND TAKE WHAT IS RIGHTFULLY YOURS!

"THANK GOD FOR SUPERNATURAL OVERFLOW INTO EVERY AREA OF YOUR LIFE NOW! THANK YOU GOD FOR REMOVING THE ENEMY SPIRIT FROM YOUR LIFE NOW!

THANK YOU GOD FOR UNLOCKING NEW CREATIVE SOLUTIONS AND MIRACLES INTO YOUR LIFE NOW!

THANK YOU GOD FOR NEW LEVELS OF PROSPERITY AND BLESSINGS ON EVERY LEVEL AND EVERY LAYER NOW!

THANK YOU GOD THANK YOU GOD THANK YOU GOD!"

Testimonial 11:
Healed From Schamberg's Disease

I had a condition at the bottom of my leg. It was always very inflamed, crimson red and extremely painful. I had gone to the doctor many times over a two-year period. It wouldn't go away. Even wearing my soft fuzzy slippers would cause pain as the fur touched the inflamed area. After the two years he did a biopsy. It was diagnosed as Schamberg's Disease. The doctor told me that there was no cure and that it would spread and could show up anywhere on my body. This was in December.

Well, as I drove home, I was adamant and decided IM NOT ACCEPTING THAT!!! I had attended several of Tracy L Clark's Body Regeneration events and workshops and had learned some of the tools and techniques to apply to the body. I connected to God and used the Body Regeneration techniques. I spoke into the body, with conviction, releasing the issue and attachments and bringing in complete healing and restoration. I also had one of Tracy's scarfs that she blesses with divine healing and wrapped it around my leg. I wore it to bed for two weeks as well as continue to apply the tools.

My husband and I were going to Mexico that January (approx. 5 weeks later) and I wanted this completely gone. I put a date and time frame for this to take place. By January when we left for our trip, it was completely gone. It has been four years now and it has not come back at all. Thank you God, Thank you Tracy!!!

E. Schneider

Allow Miracles to Unfold in Your Life
by embracing the energies of the
following testimonials:

Paying it Forward

Hi Tracy,

Where do I start?

Tracy has changed our lives, and I can't wait to change others. Mat and I have been on the Miraculous Academy Partnership programme and Body Regen 1 and 2. Every day, you get videos that you don't ever think would relate to your day, and then BAM, you understand. I have always been worried about everything, and would question why things happen and what the outcome would be if I did something differently. Tracy firstly helps you to focus on you, which I had forgotten; I would always focus on making others happy, and forget about my own happiness and wellbeing.

So as a child, I came from a broken home, and my dad chose not to make an effort to see me. I was also constantly compared to my cousin (who was in my class) by teachers and family, and out of 7 cousins, I was the only one not to go on to university. Instead, I went into the catering industry and threw myself into training to join the Royal Navy as a chef. I fell for a friend whom I had met on a cadet course, and we were together for nearly 5 years, and we were planning a future with children in the picture. I gave up my career plan so he could join as a submariner. One day, he told me that he had been cheating on me for over a year and had got a girl pregnant. After this, I threw myself back into work as a chef in training, doing 90+ hrs a week. I sustained an injury which took the doctors and consultants over a year to diagnose, and then another year to get an operation to confirm that I had ruptured the ligaments in my foot, and that I had chipped bones. I hobbled around on crutches and painkillers for a year while holding a full time job, and was told that it may be able to be fixed but would cost me by having over 6 months off work, which I couldn't afford.

I met Mat, who is my soul mate and my best friend, when I was going through all of this, and we were introduced to Tracy and the TLC Community. I was taught to do work on my body to heal the damage. And to be honest, at first, I was very sceptical; and because I was, I didn't see a difference, so I made a jump to Trust, Know, and Believe that I could fix it myself using the tools that Tracy had given me, and over time I was able to walk further, run faster, and hop, skip, and jump! And that has turned my life around!

Without this, I couldn't go to work with children as a Teaching Assistant. Now, I work with a 4-year-old boy who has challenging behaviour and is very violent towards his classmates and teachers. Since I have been there, I have been able to do Body Regen on him and myself to align us to each other and the teachers, who have known him since he started school. They have noticed a massive difference in his behaviour and, the main thing for me, his happiness. I wouldn't have noticed my real dreams until I met Tracy; she has opened my heart up for a mass of opportunity, and I can't wait for everything to come our way!

Thank you, Tracy, for your amazing work.

Thank you, God x3.

Even better x3.

Love, Bethan

The Freedom to be Me!

This is probably the toughest and easiest thing for me to do. Toughest, because I have to be vulnerable in sharing my journey. Sharing how difficult a physical symptom made me. How it prevented me from stepping into my true self. Easiest, because it is with great joy that I'm able to write this (and should have a long time ago).

I've had very severe acne, since I was 13 years old. I had painful cystic acne, blackheads, whiteheads (ALL OF IT). If I was lucky I might have 3 days out of a month without a new breakout (but still dealing with remnants of old). At the age of 31, I finally felt it cleared, with Tracy's help and my willingness to do the work.

It may sound vain, but my acne made me feel inadequate, and unlovable at my very core. I knew since my 20s that there was likely an association with self-hate, with anger, and especially anger towards myself and my dad (which surprised me). However, I just couldn't release it! I tried!

It wasn't until working with Tracy that I was able to! Tracy did the physical clearings for my skin and lymphatic system etc, but the biggest shift was in helping me release that anger and come to not only self-acceptance, but stepping into self-love. It was truly transformative!

I rarely get any breakouts anymore, even through pregnancy! I was so scared of reverting back to my old hormonal, toxic skin, but it was only a whisper of what I had in the past. Now, I may get the odd breakout, usually because I've had too much sugar, and it usually goes away the very next day! THE NEXT DAY! I NEVER thought I'd ever be able to say that. To go from acne every day, to one minor, non-painful, totally manageable breakout maybe once a month. I'll take that! I know I will have even clearer skin and my scars will be healed too. That's the next step :)

I'm so grateful to Tracy for allowing me the freedom to be me, the awareness of how I was holding myself back, and the ease and grace with which I am living now!

Chelsea St Jean

My Life Has Changed in Miraculous Ways

Since meeting Tracy and joining the Miraculous Academy, my life has changed in ways I never thought possible. Her simple tools and constant support has improved my health, finances, career, and love life, and most importantly, the relationship I have with myself. Because she truly cares, she teaches you to hold the power in your own life, and to elevate yourself to live your dreams. Thanks Tracy!! I am in such gratitude to you and this wonderful community.

Xo, Brittany

Finding Happiness Finally

Before meeting Tracy, I had studied many different practices, from yoga to meditation, as well as various lifestyle and diet approaches. I had many teachers and have attended classes, retreats, and workshops— from small and local to the world-known, huge events like Tony Robbins. Although many of them helped in my development of self-awareness, I ultimately was left with a feeling that this true "happiness" continued to elude me. Tracy was able to bring it all together to help me to finally get rid of my own old programming (the story) once and for all, allowing for me to experience the Miracle Realm that I didn't know existed. So much love and gratitude to Tracy and her whole team for the truly life changing work that they are doing!

Your friend,

Kristen Engel

xo

I am Grateful for My Healing!

I am practicing restoration, regeneration in full effect . . . it is so amazing watching and actually seeing literally the progression of healing unfold in my life because of the tools learned through you Tracy L Clark

I have had the same prescription for my eyes since I was in my early twenties . . . today I had a optical appointment and my eye sight has gotten better significantly..

WOW Thank you God and Tracy for teaching us all how to restore our bodies

I was diagnosed with RA ten years ago and I cannot wait for the day I can say to everyone I know that I am healed and restored it is coming !!

I am grateful I am in healing

Teresa Van Loon

Ease, Grace, and Miracles!

Everything that has unfolded since my session with Tracy and Friday's class:

- *suppliers I really wanted to work with to source crystals from for my new online store finally came through with amazing prices for high quality crystals*

- *found a designer for my business cards and logo that is very aligned with me and the business of energy healing*

- *Instagram followers increased*

- *many new people signed up for my newsletter*

- my health condition is improving - successfully reduced medication to half dose

Couldn't be more excited and happier! :)

Thanks to Tracy!!!

Love,

Shivani Sharma

My Pain is Gone

"I am very grateful to you for all the shiftings in my pain and for the first time in decades I feel so different and vibrant. I had gotten so used to living my life in pain that I did not know any different. I have gone to so many places and done so many modalities to get rid of this pain. I am amazed at how quickly you were able to shift it and that too like remotely.

I guess I will be a regular caller now on the show!"

Vinita Shah

Thank You for the Miraculous Healing

"Well Tracy you did it again!!! Another one of my results came back and now my fibroids are shrinking! My Doctor and I are amazed as these have been growing for 10 years. My Doctor says keep doing what you are doing. She said she was going to tell her friend about you who is into healing and mention your live events to her. So I am thankful she BELIEVES! From no cane literally the next day after just one (my first) phone call with Tracy. My cells are healing, to my lungs being clear, fibroids are shrinking . . . no cane, my list of health ailments are finally *diminishing . . . All since Nov 28/18 doing the work and connecting with Tracy daily. I was dying a slow death until I met you. Thank you Tracy, Thank you God!!"*

Sandra Pashayan

I Could Feel the Anger Leaving

I loved loved the Body Regeneration class #4!! I had a scar on my right index finger- mid area- resulting from a cut I experienced when I was 13. I never liked touching that finger- it was always tender to me, even at the age of 44. During the class today- as I was doing the exercises from Tracy in releasing the accumulation of the energy in them- I could feel energy leaving and I was not afraid to touch it. I could feel what felt like anger at that age that I had been feeling. The scar- no exaggeration looks like it has healed tremendously in seconds!!! I'm just so happy and grateful to you Tracy!!!Thank you God and Tracy!

Karen Virdi

The Doctors are Confused!

This week you did the video on eyes. I had just been to the dentist and eye doctor for check-ups and my old past cavity has disappeared . . . the dentist was so confused lol and my eyes are reversing and I was told not to wear my glasses because hey are now too strong!!! I'll take that! Thank you God!

Shannon Hoover

My Neck is Healed!

Tracy,

I just wanted to thank you for such an amazing day yesterday . . . so many lessons and tools, so much cleaning and clearing . . . I left feeling the lightest I have in years.

But a special heart-felt note of thanks for the alignment you performed on my neck.

Since I left my abusive marriage 9 years ago, I have not been able to move my neck very far to the left or to the right. I always believed it blocked bc it was too painful to look back and I was too filled with fear to look forward in my life to my next relationship.

After you adjusted me, I am literally pain free and able to move my neck with unencumbered movement.

You really are an angel sent from heaven. Thank you!! Sending hugs and heart-felt gratitude, Tracy!!

XOXO

Shelagh McGrogan

Having the Tools to Create My Next Chapters

When I came to Tracy I was looking for results, specifically for health and career/finances. Over the years I am grateful to say we have accomplished them better than I had dreamed, including new real estate, career promotions, restored health, paid off school debt, and from no savings to having our investments increase 5x in the last 2 years.

Most importantly, even though these blessings and results are what can first draw us to do this work . . . The real gift I received was a new awareness, mindset and the tools to continue to create my next chapters, to overcome any new challenges and all within a community of people who are so supportive. The true gift of working with Tracy is strengthening your own connection and learning the tools to empower each of us to do the work ourselves, in our lives, each day.

Vanessa M

Loving My Lightness of Being and Joy

The October weekend event was just AMAZING! I always love these weekends because they help me to shift a lot of what I need to shift. The energy of the last workshop was different—way more powerful! Tracy had a big shift herself the week before, and she just passed that to all of us who attended the event.

Often, after one of these weekend events, I normally can't drive. This time, I drove back for 6 hours, with a smile on my face. It's as if the new energy took place in lightness. It is really what I have been feeling since the workshop: lightness, joy, and trust in what is coming next. Now I get up earlier in the morning, with gratitude as my first thought. I'm smiling and humming often (even when I'm doing the dishes!). I'm joking more; I feel the lightness in me.

During the weekend, Tracy spoke about what my fiancé and I are preparing to do. Having the opportunity to say it in front of the group, with such strength, allowed the energy inside of me to take another step. I felt so much energy and shivers running through my body at that moment; something was cleaned and reinforced. Now it is much stronger in me, and I KNOW deeply that all is coming way quicker than I had ever thought possible. I know all will take place at the right moment, and fast. It's happening! There are a lot of things to do to get there, and after the weekend, I have way more energy. I can accomplish 1 1/2 days' worth of work in just one day, I am more efficient, and I can work longer because I have that new light energy that allows me to keep going. I love it. And I love that new level of lightness and joy.

I try to attend every event that I can, despite the 8-hour drive, because I gain so much and my life improves in incredible ways.

Thank you, Tracy, for everything, for what you are doing for all of us, and for being who you are.

You are a blessing in my life.

Bianca Cousineau

Miracles in Under 24 Hours!

Hey Tracy!!

The lump in my throat lasted most of the night. I was restless and couldn't sleep. My little sister's cat was missing in Pickering and my mind was all over the place . . . .like drifting, not scattered. Then I got a message from her in the middle of the night that she had found her cat and he has a broken leg. She was at the emergency vet. I instantly sent $200 to her. I have never sent my sister money. We don't exchange money between sisters and we don't ask. She had just bought a house, she going through a divorce and I knew her budget did not have space for an emergency vet bill. Thank you for reminding me of the beautiful gift of giving!

Two weekends ago, I had to ask my son to move out. It was a difficult truth to come to that I no longer enjoyed living with him. He will be 21 in August but I struggled to let go. He was not at all receptive to moving out and was furious when I told him and he stormed out of the house!

I hadn't heard from him since except one nasty text. At your workshop this past weekend, you asked us to write down on the back of our cards our wishes. My number one wish was to heal this situation with my son.

He just stopped by, out of the blue and we talked. We cried and we hugged and we agreed that we would take this step together. He understood that this was a difficult transition for me and agreed to come for dinner once a week, we would still hike together regularly and he would stay in touch very often to help me transition! LOL My sweet boy!

So my first wish was answered . . . truly miraculously . . . in about 16 hours!!

I have so much love for you and everyone at Team Tracy!!! Thank you God!

Kristen

Trust, Know, Believe!

Prior to attending Tracy's weekend event I was at an all time low. Things happened that I didn't think I had the strength to get through. Life was so unfair and I just couldn't do it anymore. I was ready to give up. A voice in my head kept telling me to sign up for the weekend workshop but I would ignore. It came to a point where I didn't want to be "here" anymore and again Tracy's weekend workshop just kept coming up so I reluctantly signed up for it. Up till the morning of the event I didn't want to go but something inside pushed me to get there. I am so happy that I went because it was exactly what I needed. I left there transformed. From sharing space with an amazing group of people to the shifts we received from Tracy, it was beyond powerful. I am so much at peace now and filled with gratitude. I am able to see the miracle blessings in the simplest of things every day. There's been so many triggers recently but for the first time in my life I'm unaffected by most of it. And if I do get triggered, I don't stay in it very long. It's actually really strange how calm and at peace I am. Tracy is truly amazing and is such a huge blessing in my life. My foundation, my connection to God and my faith are so much stronger. Now it's a matter of timing until all my wishes come true and I have no doubt that they will soon! Trust, know, believe!

Ria S

Printed in Great Britain
by Amazon